Trading Currency Cross Rates

Gary Klopfenstein
Jon Stein

Series Editor: Perry J. Kaufman

John Wiley & Sons, Inc.
New York • Chichester • Brisbane • Toronto • Singapore

Publisher: Karl Weber
Editor: Myles C. Thompson
Managing Editor: Linda Indig
Composition: Publications Development Company

This text is printed on acid-free paper.

This publication is designed to provide accurate and authoritative
information in regard to the subject matter covered. It is sold
with the understanding that the publisher is not engaged in
rendering legal, accounting, or other professional services. If
legal advice or other expert assistance is required, the services
of a competent professional person should be sought. FROM A
DECLARATION OF PRINCIPLES JOINTLY ADOPTED BY A COMMITTEE OF THE
AMERICAN BAR ASSOCIATION AND A COMMITTEE OF PUBLISHERS.

Library of Congress Cataloging-in-Publication Data:

Klopfenstein, Gary.
    Trading currency cross rates / Gary Klopfenstein and Jon Stein.
        p.   cm. — (Wiley traders library)
    Includes index.
    ISBN 0-471-56948-8
    1. Foreign exchange futures. 2. Hedging (Finance) I. Stein,
Jon. II. Title. III. Series.
HG3853.K58 1993
332.64'5—dc20   93-20090

Printed in the United States of America

10 9 8 7 6 5 4 3 2 1

To Candice, for all your love and support.
G.K.

To Cathy J., for your endless patience.
J.S.

ACKNOWLEDGMENTS

This book could never have been written without the help and support of many people. Special thanks should be extended to some of the vendors, academics, and businesspersons who went beyond the call of duty in helping us. These would include Paul Klopfenstein, Vice President of Foreign Exchange Trading at GK Capital Management, Inc., for his numerous ideas and insight into the markets, and David Abramson and his associates at the Bank Credit Analyst Publications Ltd. not only for their charts but for their patience with our elementary-level questions about the connections between economic indicators and the currencies markets. Thanks also to Pat Hyland at the Chicago office of Telerate, and to Dick Wallace, at First Chicago, who spent a great deal of time explaining the advantages of the cash market to those in the futures camp, and added to our understanding of interbank trading.

Another group of people who deserve credit are those who served as research analysts at GK Capital Management while this book was being written: Colin Fitzgerald, John Stevens, Leighanne Daley, Bill Rassano, Cliff Dunteman, Lisa Buccaro, and Tiffany Bullock. Their work was invaluable—examining price models, systems design, and other qualitative work.

In addition, we thank Diane Sheckler for all her work compiling, typing, and editing. Other people in the foreign exchange business who provided help include John Floyd, Karen Schotter, Kim Bang, and Alan Romney.

G.K.

J.S.

THE TRADER'S ADVANTAGE SERIES PREFACE

The Trader's Advantage Series is a new concept in publishing for traders and analysts of futures, options, equity, and generally all world economic markets. Books in the series present single ideas with only that background information needed to understand the content. No long introductions, no definitions of the futures contract, clearing house, and order entry. Focused.

The futures and options industry is no longer in its infancy. From its role as an agricultural vehicle it has become the alterego of the most active world markets. The use of EFPs (exchange for physicals) in currency markets makes the selection of physical or futures markets transparent, in the same way the futures markets evolved into the official pricing vehicle for world grain. With a single telephone call, a trader or investment manager can hedge a stock portfolio, set a crossrate, perform a swap, or buy the protection of an inflation index. The classic regimes can no longer be clearly separated.

And this is just the beginning. Automated exchanges are penetrating traditional open outcry markets. Even now, from the time the transaction is completed in the pit, everything else is electronic. "Program trading" is the automated response to the analysis of a computerized ticker tape, and it is just the tip of the inevitable evolutionary process. Soon the executions will be computerized and then we won't be able to call anyone to complain about a fill. Perhaps we won't even have to place an order to get a fill.

Market literature has also evolved. Many of the books written on trading are introductory. Even those intended for more advanced audiences often include a review of contract specifications and market mechanics. There are very few books specifically targeted for the experienced and professional traders and analysts. *The Trader's Advantage Series* changes all that.

This series presents contributions by established professionals and exceptional research analysts. The authors' highly specialized talents have been applied primarily to futures, cash, and equity markets but are often generally applicable to price forecasting. Topics in the series will include trading systems and individual techniques, but all are a necessary part of the development process that is intrinsic to improving price forecasting and trading.

These works are creative, often state-of-the-art. They offer new techniques, in-depth analysis of current trading methods, or innovative and enlightening ways of looking at still unsolved problems. The ideas are explained in a clear, straightforward manner with frequent examples and illustrations. Because they do not contain unnecessary background material they are short and to the point. They require careful reading, study, and consideration. In exchange, they contribute knowledge to help build an unparalleled understanding of all areas of market analysis and forecasting.

PERRY J. KAUFMAN

FOREWORD

Gary Klopfenstein and Jon Stein have written a wonderfully informative and readable explanation of the biggest of all world markets—cross rates. While foreign exchange is familiar to everyone, a cross rate is a perceptual problem in many countries, but especially in the U.S. As the authors explain, "Every exchange rate is a cross rate." Each country views exchange rates through their own eyes. To a Japanese trader, the U.S. dollar is the dollar/yen rate; to a Frankfurt businessman, the Swedish rate is the Krona/Deutsche mark.

Thinking of the mark, lira, sterling, yen, won, peso, or renminbi only in terms of the U.S. dollar limits trading opportunities to a small fraction of the market. Large transactions occur between major trading partners, often referred to as "blocs." Exchange rates within these blocs vary due to the balance of trade and economic health of the participating countries. Although the U.S. dollar may be weakening with respect to all European bloc nations, the British pound may itself be trading lower against the Deutsche mark. These relationships become clear when seen from the right perspective, and uncertain when separated and expressed as sterling/dollar and Deutsche mark/dollar rates.

This global view of the foreign exchange market opens opportunities for highly liquid trading and added portfolio diversification. It can be done without seeking obscure new markets and struggling with unreliable data.

Gary Klopfenstein and Jon Stein have taken a very practical approach. Even if you are familiar with cross rates, you will gain new insights and comfort from their examples. They combine straight-forward explanations of relevant factors and clear technical analysis of prices. In addition to the highly active interbank arbitrage, the authors discuss how to apply 24-hour markets, without the normal open, high, low, and closing quotes, to technical trading.

Currency trading is most active between major trading partners, and these relationships continue to change. This presents challenges and opportunities. Even during the writing of this book, the group structure that defines the European Monetary System has been altered. The former Soviet Union is fragmented, each part seeking its own avenues of trade. At this time, *The Wall Street Journal* does not quote any exchange rate for the Commonwealth of Independent States (CIS), or its individual entities. But these countries are an important part of U.S. trade and will affect the value of the dollar. For now, it may only be possible to track CIS activity as a cross rate between its other trading partners, Germany and China. For both simple and specialized situations, you'll find this book very helpful.

PERRY J. KAUFMAN

Wells River, Vermont

PREFACE

This book has been the culmination of a great deal of work over one and a half years. We set out in the beginning to write a book dealing with cross rate trading in currencies. Because this area is constantly evolving, the text and chart examples have been revised many times. We have tried to make the examples apply over a broad range of markets and currencies. The result is a text that touches on many areas and has many applications. Undoubtably, changes will occur in the economics of the world currency markets as time passes, most likely even before this book is published. Nevertheless, even though some examples in this text may no longer appear up to date, the concepts behind them should still retain their relevance. The analysis we provide should be applicable to different markets and market situations in the ever-changing foreign exchange arena.

We wrote this book to fill a gap in existing literature between the basic primers on futures trading and the complicated texts on currency pricing models and the like. *Trading Currency Cross Rates* is designed to fall somewhere in between. We have tried to gear it toward readers who have some experience trading futures or options, perhaps even as trading advisors or trading managers, and who are looking to trade either in the cash market or cross rates, or both. Consequently, we assume that readers have some knowledge of trading and market terms.

A problem that became evident over the past few years is that there is not at this time an effective way to trade currency cross rates in the futures markets. Some futures contracts exist, but they lack the liquidity for moderate-size traders. Futures and options traders, as a result, are unable to take full advantage of the international currency markets. So the book also became a text dealing with switching from the futures market into the cash currency market. This is a switch that I (G.K.) made in my own trading in 1989 and have found to be both challenging and profitable. We hope that you will have the same experience.

In explaining the transition from futures to interbank and from dollar-based exchange rates to cross rates, many topics come to mind. This text explores the most important topics. Two topics—options trading in the interbank market and regulatory and tax consequences—were not included because the topics could constitute a book in itself. We are confident that what lies between these two covers "delivers the goods."

GARY KLOPFENSTEIN
JON STEIN

CONTENTS

1

INTRODUCING CROSS RATES AND THE INTERBANK MARKET

Although several books have been written about the foreign exchange cash market, very few explain how to trade it. Even fewer—almost none, actually—mention currency cross rates. In the currency futures markets, cross rates seem to be treated as some kind of new phenomenon. In the cash market (a term that covers spot, forwards, swaps, and OTC options), cross rates are neither new nor an interesting little "corner" of the market. They *are* the currency market, plain and simple. An interesting headline appeared in the markets section of *The Wall Street Journal* on June 8, 1992: "Dollar Is Narrowly Mixed, the Fed Sells Marks for Lire on Behalf of Bank of Italy." Even some seasoned currency traders probably wondered what business our Federal Reserve had in helping to realign currencies of the European Monetary System.

The reader of this text should realize two things cash traders already know: one, cross rates are as important as dollar-based rates, and two, every exchange rate is a cross rate.

Before explaining what cross rates are and where to trade them, it is crucial to understand the difference between a "currency" and an "exchange rate." Currencies are actual units priced in terms of other units. While the difference seems simple enough, many a floor trader in Chicago believe they are quoting Japanese yen itself, rather than Japenese yen in terms of U.S. dollars.

WHAT IS A CROSS RATE?

Any two currencies can be part of an exchange transaction. The term *cross rate* is actually rather parochial since it has traditionally served as a convenient way for nationals of a particular country to describe currency exchange rates between *other* countries. For instance, some-one living in France would consider mark-yen to be a cross rate while mark-French might not be. Every exchange rate is a cross rate because it is one currency expressed in terms of another. So, although cross rate describes any exchange rate, or at least any exchange rate between two nonnative currencies, today North Americans use the term essentially to describe transactions that do not involve the dollar. Of course, a "cross rate" may even raise eyebrows of confused European or Asian counterparts. It is for the purposes of clarity, not ethnocentrism, that this text will refer to non-dollar-based exchange rates as cross rates.

Nearly everyone who has ever picked up a copy of *The Wall Street Journal* has at least seen the term. The markets section, in fact, reserves space for a small box titled "Key Cross Rates," stating what particular currencies are worth in other currencies. Figure 1–1 shows the table provided to the *Journal* by Telerate, for November 10, 1992.

The interbank market solves any problem in terminology by calling each exchange rate by its component currencies. In this book, we have done something that may look strange at first to an American trader—every exchange rate is hyphenated. The value of the currency before the hyphen rises when the level of that exchange rate rises, while the ups and downs are denominated in terms of the currency after the hyphen. "Mark-peseta," for example, describes the Deutsche mark quoted in terms of Spanish peseta; "mark-peseta is dropping" would describe the mark dropping against the peseta or the peseta rising against the mark. Likewise, "Swiss-yen" is Swiss francs priced in Japanese yen. The only anomaly may be the stubborn habit of some dealers in referring to British pounds quoted in dollars as "dollar-sterling" even though they are quoted and followed as "sterling-dollar."

Key Currency Cross Rates   Late New York Trading Nov. 10, 1992

	Dollar	Pound	SFranc	Guilder	Yen	Lira	D-Mark	FFranc	CdnDlr
Canada	1.2645	1.9163	.88180	.70493	.01019	.00093	.79304	.23478	....
France	5.3860	8.162	3.7559	3.0026	.04338	.00397	3.3779	....	4.2594
Germany	1.5945	2.4165	1.1119	.88890	.01284	.00117	....	.29605	1.2610
Italy	1357.5	2057.3	946.65	756.77	10.934	....	851.36	252.04	1073.5
Japan	124.15	188.15	86.576	69.211	....	.09145	77.861	23.051	98.18
Netherlands ...	1.7938	2.7185	1.2509	....	.01445	.00132	1.1250	.33305	1.4186
Switzerland	1.4340	2.1732	....	.79942	.01155	.00106	.89934	.26625	1.1340
U.K.	.65985	....	.46015	.36785	.00531	.00049	.41383	.12251	.52183
U.S.	....	1.5155	.69735	.55748	.00805	.00074	.62716	.18567	.79083

Source: Telerate

Figure 1–1   Cross-Rate Table as Provided by Telerate. *(Source: Wall Street Journal)*

In other words, a quote in pounds of 1.65 means that there are 1.65 dollars in a pound. However, the same quote in dollar-mark would mean that there are 1.65 marks in a dollar. The reason for this is just that it has always been done this way, and it is difficult to change at this juncture. Currencies that are actively traded and quoted backward are the pound and Australian dollar.

The first question to consider about cross rates is, How can you play the rate between two foreign currencies without jumping into one or the other first? If you want to buy marks with yen, don't you buy yen first and thus expose yourself to the rate between yen and your home currency? The answer is no. The procedure for entering the cross rate depends on your home currency, but the quote between the mark and the yen is always treated the same, wherever you are. U.S.-based traders, for instance, playing the mark-yen rate, are usually first told their bank's current bid-ask for the cross, say 85.65-85.76 DM/JY. A request for dollar-based quotes in the two currencies would obtain the following: a dollar-mark of, say, 1.5180-1.5190 DM/$, and dollar-yen of, say 130.10-130.20 JY/$. Dividing the first of these by the second should yield the quoted mark-yen rate (130.10/1.5190 = 85.65; 130.20/1.5180 = 85.76). For the American trader, the cross rate (85.76 if buying the cross) is usually just shorthand for two dollar-based transactions. The same principle would apply to an Italian, Australian, or any other trader whose home currency is something other than the mark or the yen. When the home currency is one of the target currencies, mark or yen, the transaction is a simple exchange.

In the interbank market, accordingly the account balance and profit/loss figures are usually denominated either in the trader's home currency or the U.S. dollar. The only time this would not be the case would be when the trader for some reason wants to take delivery, after the trade is liquidated, in one of the foreign currencies. Some corporations desire this for various economic and accounting reasons; most trading advisors, however, do not.

POPULARITY

According to the Bank of International Settlements, the quantity of reported interbank currency transactions on an average day in early 1992 hovered around US$ 500 billion. By the end of 1992, estimates had risen to over US$ 600 billion. Cross-currency rates accounted for a much larger portion of this volume than most currency futures traders might have realized. In the New York interbank market, cross rates make up roughly 35% of total volume. In the European money center, London, for example, the figure is closer to 45%. The second most popular exchange rate traded in the world is a cross rate—the mark-yen—just after the dollar-mark exchange rate. After mark-yen, the next most popular cross rates are the sterling-mark and the mark-Swiss.

Some cross rates are more volatile than others. As explained in Chapter 3, certain cross rates, such as those between the D-mark and other member currencies of the exchange rate mechanism (ERM) of the European Monetary System—mark-guilder for example (D-marks in Dutch guilders)—can be downright sleepy as they maintain predetermined, static boundaries. There were some claims that the once-bouncy sterling-mark exchange rate had also fallen victim to this phenomenon. But as we will see later, volatility has returned to the European Monetary System (EMS). In any case, the central banks of European countries, specifically EMS members, are much more likely to intervene in the currency markets than their U.S. or Canadian counterparts. Central banks affect currency valuations either by direct intervention into the market or by playing with interest rates. In the United States, where the Federal Reserve exercises both less frequently than do the European centers, traders have become used to economic conditions—inflation, unemployment, and so on—as explanations of Fed activity. In addition to economic conditions, European central bankers also worry about which rung on the EMS ladder their currency occupies. These centers will intervene and, sometimes, affect interest rate changes to pull their currency up from the lower end of the range vis-à-vis another currency. Figure 1–2 shows the intervention limits for the EMS currencies as of October 1992.

This figure lists current spot rates, as well as the intervention limits. If the currency goes outside these limits, the central bank of that country is obligated to take steps, via interest rate changes or intervention, to move the currency back inside its bounds. At the time of this writing, the British pound and Italian lira have suspended their participation in the ERM.

Traders can also compare the dollar markets with what's happening in the cross rates. Sometimes movement in the dollar will seem to coincide with the movement of another exchange rate; at other times, it appears completely disconnected. Figures 1–3 through 1–5 present daily bar charts for mark-yen, French-yen, and dollar-yen. The mark and French charts are very similar, while the dollar chart takes a slightly different course. Several important lessons that can be learned from these charts, but we will save that discussion for the section on intermarket analysis in Chapter 5.

EMS CURRENCIES	LATEST SPOT RATE	CENTRAL PARITY & INTERVENTION LIMITS vs. DM		
		Upper Limit	Central Parity	Lower Limit
Belgian Franc	20.550	21.095	20.626	20.166
Danish Krone	3.8332	3.9016	3.8144	3.7300
Dutch Guilder	1.1238	1.1524	1.1267	1.1017
French Franc	3.3879	3.4305	3.3539	3.2792
Irish Punt	2.6109	2.6190	2.6789	2.7400
Italian Lira (suspended)	863.26			
Portuguese Escudo	89.130	92.340	86.940	81.900
Spanish Peseta	70.686	72.622	68.421	64.430
British Pound (susp.)	2.4425			

Figure 1–2 European Market System Currencies with Central Parity Levels, Upper and Lower Intervention Boundaries, as of November 1, 1992.

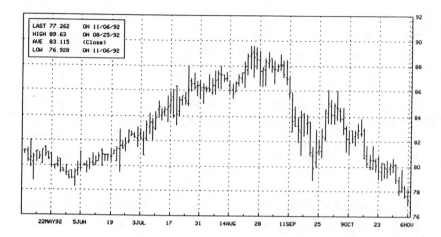

Figure 1–3 **Mark-Yen, Daily Chart from May 11, 1992, to November 6, 1992.**
(*Source:* Bloomberg L.P.)

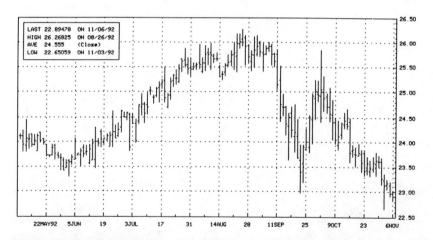

Figure 1–4 **French-Yen, Daily Chart from May 11, 1992, to November 6, 1992.**
(*Source:* Bloomberg L.P.)

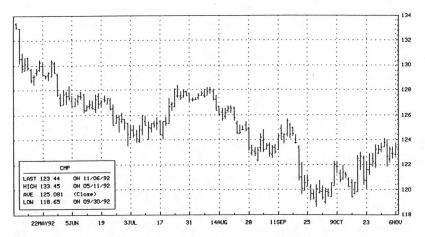

CMP	
LAST 123.44	ON 11/06/92
HIGH 133.45	ON 05/11/92
AVE 125.081	(Close)
LOW 118.65	ON 09/30/92

Figure 1–5   Dollar-Yen, Daily Chart from May 11, 1992, to November 6, 1992.
(*Source:* **Bloomberg L.P.**)

THE OTHER SIDE OF THE TRADE

Traders looking to make the switch from the futures market to the cash market will ask, Who is taking the other side of a cash currency trade? Similarly, on the floors of both the stock exchange and the futures exchanges, there is always much talk about who is on the other side of the trade. Every post on the New York Stock Exchange has a specialist, or holder of the "book" of customer buy and sell orders entered by the large wire houses, whose telephone lines constantly buzz with information on the size of the book or the entity behind the latest large order. Similarly, on the floor of most U.S. futures exchanges, and some European ones, a person known as a local, gives a two-way market on the current contract, making money off the difference between bid and ask. There are also brokers who represent other speculators' orders. In either case, the order of a speculator buying at the current market could be filled by the person making the market or by a broker representing another speculator who's selling.

In the interbank market, when a large speculator calls up a bank to buy or sell a currency, the bank will quote a bid-offer spread. In reality, the bank is usually taking the other side of the trade. The bank may keep this position for itself if the bank trader believes that the position will be profitable, and hence, that the speculator's position is unprofitable. Otherwise, the bank will offset the trade by executing the offsetting trade with another customer of the bank. So, the bank is either adding to its position in the market or immediately exiting the position. When banks exit, they are generally able to do so at a profit. For example, if a bank is quoting dollar-mark at 1.6525 bid, 1.6530 offered, they will sell dollars to a customer at 1.6530. They can then simultaneously buy them from another customer who wishes to sell at 1.6525. So the banks have the best of both worlds. If they have a sufficient volume of business, they can either hold the position for themselves or profit from the bid-ask spread. This type of trading has recently been a major source for profits at banks.

It is also possible that the bank is not taking the other side of the trade. Whether or not they are taking the other side of the trade depends on whether they are taking the role of principal or agent in the transaction. If they are principal, then they are the counterparty to the trade. However, if they are agent, then they will find another party to take the opposite side. Almost without exception, banks and currency brokers are operating as principals, so they are the counterparty to the trade. On the other hand, many traditional futures brokerage firms operate on an agency basis in the cash currency markets. In an agency relationship, the speculator will call for a quote. The bank or brokerage firm then will call another bank, or several banks to obtain the best price. Once a price to buy or sell is established, the agent bank will then quote the price to the speculator. If the speculator wants to trade at the given price, the agent bank will then buy from the principal bank for the customer. As a result, the agent bank is never actually taking a position for itself.

The advantage of dealing with an agent is that the agent is not the counterparty and can try to get the best possible price for the trader. On the other hand, a bank that acts as principal is taking the other side of the trade, and tries to get the best possible price for itself. So there is a conflict of interest in trading with a bank that is acting as principal. So the question might be posed, Why trade with a bank or broker when it is acting as principal? The answer is speed of execution. Principal banks are able to quote a price immediately, whereas agents must first find a counterparty. Many traders feel that they might as well call principal banks themselves as have an agent bank do it for them. The end result, is that the necessary speed of execution and the relationship between the trader and the bank desk are the two factors that should determine whether to trade on an agency or principal basis.

In the interbank currency markets, a trader calls a broker-dealer or bank to get a market. But the backbone and the liquidity of the currency markets come from the various commercial transactions whose origins have little to do with currencies. A company in England, for example, that offers its product to a German retailer will sell the product at a price that is fixed today—but maybe not at today's exchange rate. In fact, the exchange rate will most likely be fixed on delivery, say in three months. If the payment is made in D-marks, the seller carries an exposure to an adverse—in this case upward—movement in the sterling-mark cross rate. In other words, the seller may be paid with D-marks that are not worth as much in pounds as they were when the sale was made. Therefore, the seller would go into the foreign exchange markets and hedge its exposure by buying sterling-mark, that is, selling D-marks in favor of British pounds (in this case, the seller's home currency). This type of transaction is carried out frequently, not just between British and German businesses but with all sorts of trading partners—and U.S. dollars are never involved. Such transactions are the reason for the enormous liquidity of the currency markets.

DERIVATIVES

Ask any manager in the foreign exchange department of a large bank what their largest growth area will be for the 1990s and they'll most likely answer quickly, "Options." They are talking, not about exchange-traded options, but about over-the-counter (OTC) options. These options on cash foreign exchange are to exchange-traded options on currency futures what cash foreign exchange is to currency futures. The over-the-counter options market has been, and will continue to be, fueled largely by bank customers hedging their currency risk. But now speculators are catching on as well. The interbank OTC options market has come a long way in the past 10 years, offering corporations, institutional investors, and anyone else with foreign exchange exposures some creative approaches to hedging that risk. The transaction of the British manufacturer in the preceding example, which carries a risk of depreciating German currency before payment, could also be hedged by buying a put option: a contract for the right to sell D-marks at a specific price at expiration of the option. Because both the price and expiration are at the customer's discretion, the option market offers a great deal of flexibility.

In this case, the manufacturer would most likely structure the option to keep the price at the current level and the expiration date the same date as the date of the delivery of goods.

These approaches will be familiar to readers who are well-versed in options trading. This text will not delve into the various pricing formulas for OTC option contracts or discuss options theory at any length. We assume that the futures trader or investment advisor with an affinity for options can use them as instruments to achieve a desired directional or market volatility play and that, to accomplish this, the OTC market is their arena. Traders interested in OTC options are even more encouraged by the efforts most banks are now putting into marketing their OTC services toward speculative clients.

2

Exchange-Traded versus Interbank Markets

Before becoming immersed in the strategies and tactics in the currency cross rate markets, traders must realize that much depends on the type of trading vehicle used. This text presents two basic ideas: what a cross rate is and the different kinds of cross rates that exist. Right now, you may be more interested in getting to the heart of the matter: clarifying the best methods for forecasting moves in cross rates and finding out what money-making strategies and tactics exist. However, before talking about analysis or strategy, it is important to decide whether, as a trader, you plan to trade the exchange instruments such as futures or the cash market, or both.

FOREIGN EXCHANGE AND THE FUTURES MARKETS

Any trader serious about seeking out opportunities in the cross rate arena must first realize the demands and limitations of both the cash market and the futures market, and then weigh these characteristics against assorted strategies available in each arena. Overall, the futures market, offers much less variety and enjoys less volume. A choice of one or the other—or both—greatly depends on the volume the trader desires and financial capacity of the trader, and sometimes the trader's background as well.

To depict the futures market as some kind of second-choice alternative to the cash market would be grossly unfair. Although currency futures volume constitutes barely 1% of the total foreign exchange volume done in U.S. banks alone on a given day, this blurs the real picture. The futures markets thrive because the banks not only like them, but need them. This was illustrated in the early 1980s by the role the futures markets played in expanding both the hedging business from investment banks and the arbitrage trading by commercial banks themselves. By tradition, the interbank market has been a much more exclusive club than it is today. Only recently have the largest investment banks in North America been allowed in to trade as counterparties; for the most part they had been shut out. As the degree of the U.S. investment banks' underwriting and offering activities in other countries increased, so did their currency exposure. One solution was to expand their rather limited currency execution desks into actual banklike trading operations. The institutions that make up the interbank market, however, viewed Wall Street firms as too risky to serve as counterparties (perhaps not such an unfair perception on the eve of the Drexel debacle), although they were more than welcome as regular customers. These firms turned to the futures markets instead for their hedging needs. What soon followed was enormous amounts of buying in the futures markets, which often pushed the various contract prices above their theoretical differential (often referred to as "basis") with interbank spot prices. Such discrepancies created many opportunities to arbitrage—to capture profits for little or no risk—between the futures and cash. An era of "free money" existed for awhile as the investment houses themselves and the few banks that would do business with them, mostly Chicago-based institutions such as Harris Trust and First Chicago, cashed in by selling futures contracts and buying their interbank counterparts. Ironically, most of the larger, New York banks didn't catch on until the arbitrage play had largely disappeared and the futures began trading in line with spot. Today, a number of investment banks such as Morgan Stanley and Merrill Lynch trade in the interbank market as counterparties. So, as the markets have become more developed, the interbank market has recognized not only the importance of the exchange as an alternative to its own market, but as a source of arbitrage opportunities.

Many futures traders dismiss out-of-hand the oft-touted advantages of the cash foreign exchange market. They cut their teeth on the exchange markets, it's the market they know best, and that's where they will stay. Many of these traders may be truly missing out on a grand, astonishingly liquid, yet intimidating, market that has even made converts of floor traders. In fact, any trader would be severely disadvantaged by not reading the subsequent section on the interbank market. Although the structure and financial demands of the cash market probably close it off to the majority of futures and options speculators, it provides a 24-hour forum of great depth, driving price movement in other markets—most notably its corresponding futures counterparts.

For the traditional players in the interbank market, the situation is just the opposite. The arrival of cross-rate futures has gone largely without notice in the interbank market. The stalwart of this market, the multinational corporation, participates largely to purchase something using, or to hedge exposures in, a foreign currency. Not only are such firms less comfortable with the futures market, they can afford the demanding credit lines of the bank market. The financial officer calls the same bank through which the firm effects all its other transactions, to buy and sell the currencies needed. When it comes to cross-currency rates, a concept the futures exchanges are still trying to get across to their regular customers, the barriers are even higher. The lists provided in Figures 2–1 and 2–2 illustrate the breadth of the interbank market and the banks that participate in it. The ranking order of the lists shows the results of a qualitative and quantitative survey taken annually by the editors of *Euromoney* magazine and covers the 1991 survey results. Although these surveys are conducted annually, the rankings are fairly consistent, with the same banks achieving high ratings each year and few new names appearing. Since surveys of interbank traders are used to determine the rankings, they carry a lot of weight in the foreign exchange industry.

EXCHANGE-TRADED CROSS RATES

At present, exchange-traded cross rates have attracted little commercial or speculative interest. Before describing the variety, or dearth, of foreign exchange instruments available on the world's organized

Australian dollar:
1) ANZ
2) Westpac
3) Commonwealth Bank of Australia

Dutch guilder:
1) ABN
2) Amro
3) Barclays

French franc:
1) Banque Nationale de Paris
2) Societe Generale
3) Barclays

Italian lira:
1) Banca Commerciale Italiana
2) Credito Italiana
3) Instituto Bancario San Paulo di Torino

Nordic currencies:
1) SE Banken
2) Den Danske Bank
3) Den Norske Creditbank

Portugese escudo:
1) Banco Totta & Acores
2) Banco Espirito Santo
3) Banco Portgues do Atlantico

Spanish peseta:
1) Banco Bilbao Vizcaya
2) NatWest
3) Banco Hispano Americano

D-mark:
1) Deutsche Bank
2) Citicorp
3) Chemical Bank

Yen:
1) Bank of Tokyo
2) Citicorp
3) Industrial Bank of Japan

British pound:
1) Barclays
2) Citicorp
3) NatWest

Swiss franc:
1) Union Bank of Switzerland
2) Swiss Bank Corp
3) Citicorp

Figure 2–1 Best Interbank Dealers in Selected Currencies as Surveyed by Readers of *Euromoney*. (Source: *Euromoney*)

exchanges, it is necessary to qualify use of the terms *futures market* and *futures trader*. A reason exists for the use of the term *exchange instruments* rather than simply *futures and options* contracts. The problem with "futures and options" is the description's implied neglect of SEC-regulated options and warrants, two markets that act very much

Mark-yen:
1) Bank of Tokyo
2) Citibank
3) Deutsche Bank

Sterling-mark:
1) Barclays
2) Citicorp
3) Northwest

Swiss-yen:
1) Union Bank of Switz.
2) Citicorp
3) Bank of Tokyo

Mark-swiss:
1) Union Bank of Switzerland
2) Deutsche Bank
3) Swiss Bank Corp

EMS Cross-rates:
1) Deutsche Bank
2) Barclays
3) JP Morgan

Figure 2–2 Best Interbank Dealers in Selected Cross Rates as Surveyed by Readers of *Euromoney*. (Source: *Euromoney*)

like the options-on-futures markets but with much more liquidity. While the SEC-regulated instruments do not form a large bulk of exchange-traded currency products, they exist and are on the rise.

As of this writing, an estimated 37 foreign exchange-related instruments of varying liquidity currently trade on the world's securities and futures exchanges, yet scarcely one-third of them involve a cross rate, that is, an exchange rate not including the U.S. dollar. Not surprisingly, almost half of these contracts are found in the United States. A listing of these contracts can be found in Figures 2–3 and 2–4.

Probably the most prevalent class of exchange-traded cross rate instruments are futures contracts. At the exchanges where they have been initiated, currency cross-rate futures can be traded like any

Currency Country	Exchange Rate	Denomination	Point Value	Exchange
Australia	Aussie-dollar	A$ 100,000	US$0.0001/A$=US$10	SFE
Brazil	dollar-cruzeiro	US$ 5,000	Cr50	BMF
	yen-cruzeiro	Y 1,000,000	Cr50	BMF
	mark-cruzeiro	DM 10,000	Cr50	BMF
Japan	dollar-yen	US$ 50,000	0.05pt=Y 2,500	TIFFE
Netherlands	dollar-guilder	US$ 25,000	$0.05=12.50 DFL	FTA
Singapore	mark-dollar	SM 125,000	$0.0001/DM=$12.50	SIMEX
	yen-dollar	Y 12,500,000	$0.0001/Y100=$12.50	SIMEX
	sterling dollar	£ 62,500	$0.0002/BP=$12.50	SIMEX
Spain	dollar-peseta	US$ 100,000	1pt=1,000 Pta	MEFF
	mark-peseta	DM 125,000	1pt=1,250 Pta	MEFF
United Kingdom	sterling-dollar	£ 25,000	1pt=£12.50	LIFFE
	mark-dollar	DM 125,000	US$0.0001/DM=US$12.50	LIFFE
United States	mark-dollar	DM 125,000	US$0.0001/DM=$12.50	IMM
	C-dollar-dollar	C$ 100,000	US$0.0001/C$=$10.00	IMM
	swiss-dollar	SF 125,000	US$0.0001/SF=$12.50	IMM
	sterling-dollar	£ 62,500	US$0.0002/BP=$12.50	IMM
	yen-dollar	Y 12,500,000	US$0.0001/100JY=$12.50	IMM
	A-dollar-dollar	A$ 100,000	US$0.0001/A$=$10.00	IMM
	sterling-mark	US$ 50,000 x BP/DM rate	0.0005=$25	IMM
	mark-swiss	US$ 125,000 x DM/SF rate	0.0002=$25	IMM
	mark-yen	US$ 125,000 x DM/JY rate	0.0002=$25	IMM

Figure 2–3 Currency Futures Contracts Listed by Country. (*Source:* Bloomberg L.P.)

Currency Country	Exchange Rate	Denomination	Point Value	Exchange
Australia	Aussie-dollar	(see other table)		SFE
Netherlands	dollar-guilder	US$ 10,000	0.05 DFL	EOE
	dollar-guilder	US$ 100,000	0.05 DFL	EOE
	sterling-guilder	£ 10,000	0.05 DFL	EOE
Singapore	mark-dollar	(see other table)		SIMEX
	yen-dollar	(see other table)		SIMEX
United Kingdom	sterling-dollar	£ 25,000		LIFFE
	mark-dollar	US$ 50,000		LIFFE
United States	mark-dollar	DM 125,000	US$0.01/DM	IMM
	C-dollar-dollar	C$ 100,000	US$0.01/C$	IMM
	swiss-dollar	SF 125,000	US$0.01/SF	IMM
	sterling-dollar	£ 62,500	US$0.02/BP	IMM
	yen-dollar	Y 12,500,000	US$0.0001/JY	IMM
	A-dollar-dollar	A$ 100,000	US$0.01/A$	IMM
	mark-yen	DM 125,000	0.01 yen/mark	IMM
	sterling-mark	£ 31,250	0.01 mark/sterling	Phila. Stock Exchange
	mark-yen	DM 62,500	0.01 yen/mark	Phila. Stock Exchange

Figure 2–4 Currency Options Contracts Listed by Country. (*Source:* Bloomberg L.P.)

other futures contracts. At the Chicago Mercantile Exchange (CME), the trading price of each futures contract reflects the ratio between the two futures contracts on the underlying currencies, and the price at settlement is decided by those other futures prices. In other words, unlike other contracts, the CME's contracts, technically speaking, are based on other futures and not on a cash price. If CME yen futures are trading at 0.7300 $/100 yen, and D-Mark futures at 0.6250 $/DM, in theory the corresponding mark-yen cross rate future market should be around 0.8560 (0.6250 divided by 0.7300). For the most part, they work in the same way as the regular currency futures. They are settled in cash, traders must set up an account with a futures broker and set aside initial and maintenance margins, and adjustments are made to the trader's account as the market changes. The futures and options markets are usually fairly liquid arenas for executing speculative positions in foreign exchange in general and, depending on the trader's goals, often offer advantages over the cash market. Overall, such advantages currently appear to be enjoyed more by small-to-medium players than by the large players, because of liquidity constraints in the futures markets.

OPTIONS

Options are becoming an increasingly important part of foreign exchange trading. In this section, we will describe briefly the workings of the cross rate option markets and discuss some considerations for implementing them into trading models. The discussion is not intended to be an exhaustive study of option pricing or valuation, but a conceptual overview of the instruments.

Two types of options are traded on cross rates, exchange traded and over-the-counter, more commonly called OTC. The conceptual differences between the two are obvious. If an option is traded on an exchange, it may have futures contracts as the underlying instrument. On the other hand, OTC options, which are non-exchange-traded options, always have a cash currency position as the underlying instrument. OTC options are to exchange-traded options what the cash currency market is to currency futures. As of this writing, there is an enormous amount of volume daily in the OTC market, and very little on the exchanges. Consequently, we will use the OTC market for most of the illustrations. First, however, we will examine some of the history and details of both markets.

While the jury is still out as to which genre of currency options came first, exchange-traded or OTC options. Banks began quoting markets in OTC options roughly around the same time the Philadelphia exchange began courting them with its options market. At first, contracts in both markets were quoted in the premium (price) terms most stock and futures investors are used to. In the early 1980s, the OTC market introduced volatility pricing, where a buyer would be quoted a volatility percentage such as "12.8" rather than a price. At the same time, banks began selling these options to speculators, and arbitragers "delta-hedged," that is, automatically hedged with forwards or spot. In 1985, the London Interbank Currency Options Market (LICOM) was created to cover only the London clearing banks, but it quickly attracted other members. In 1992, the "London" part was dropped to form the truly international ICOM.

While an options trade may span the gamut of complexity, it always can be broken down into two components: a call option—the right to purchase one currency with another at a set exchange rate; or a put option—the right to sell one currency for another at a set rate. Holders of "American-style" options may exercise their option on any day until expiration; "European-style" options have the right to exercise their option only on the day of expiration.

Perhaps the first aspect of the options market that must be made clear to cross-rate traders concerns terminology. For example, what a U.S. trader would call a "Swiss franc call" carries the right to buy Swiss francs for dollars, but it is also a U.S. dollar put since it includes the right to sell dollars for Swiss francs. This all gets confusing when cross rates are involved. To avoid this confusion of not knowing in which currency the trader will end up long or short, European dealers often name both currencies in the option. A mark-yen option, for example, might be quoted, "Yen call, mark put, struck at 78.50, expiry March 15."

Before going much further, we should examine the similarities and differences between exchange-traded and OTC options. The similarities are easiest because there are so few of them. In general, all the basic strategies can work in either market, and both use the same valuation models. Other than that, there are mostly differences.

The first thing to consider is the instrument on which the underlying position is based. Exchange-traded currency options can be based on either the underlying futures contract or on the spot price, depending on where it is traded. The underlying instrument is the spot market if you are dealing with the Philadelphia exchange. On the other hand, options traded at the IMM have the futures market as their underlying instrument. The OTC options use the cash market. An example will show why the underlying instrument is relevant. If the dollar is trading at the equivalent of 140 yen in the spot market, but futures are at the equivalent of 138.50 $/yen, a futures-style option with 138.50 strike would be "at the money" (these include the IMM and Globex cross-rate options). This would not be the case for a 138.50 spot-based OTC option. It would be in the money if it were a call, or out of the money if it were a put.

The underlying instrument also relates to settlement. When an option in the OTC market is exercised, it is treated the same as if a spot trade had taken place. This is also the case for Philadelphia options. However, the IMM options become a futures position upon exercise. In addition, OTC options have the ability to trade as either European or American style.

The actual trading of the options in the two markets is also quite different, as evidenced by the way they are priced. Exchange-traded options are priced by premium, much like stock options. For instance, a mark call option might be priced at 0.24. This would mean that the buyer would pay $300 in premium for each 125,000 marks (1,250 × 0.24). On the other hand, OTC options are priced in terms of volatility and are generally quoted for strike prices that are at the money. For instance, a similar mark quote in the OTC market might be 6.75. This quote would mean that for each $1 million, the option premium would cost 6.75%, or $67,500. The CME has recently introduced a volatility-based pricing mechanism, although most traders on the floor are still executed via dollar pricing.

This is a good place to examine what goes into the pricing of option premiums. These premiums have three basic components: intrinsic value, time value, and volatility. Time value is a function of the interest rates in the forward market as well as the time remaining until expiry. We will assume that the reader understands these terms, and not deal with them specifically. There are several risks that traders must understand before jumping into OTC options. The first is counterparty risk. As is the case with the cash currency market, there is risk of counterparty default. If holders of a call or put that is very far in the money have a counterparty default, they will not realize the profit on that option. That is the principal reason it is difficult to find anyone to quote options with over one-year duration. One year is simply too long to be exposed to the risk. Another risk in OTC markets that traces its roots to the cash market is its lack of regulation. Because of this, the relationship with the bank becomes extremely important.

One last caution for the trader: Even though these markets are extremely liquid, there have been times when they have become nearly impossible to trade. The most notable example of this was during the turmoil in the exchange rate mechanism (ERM) in September 1992. Remember that two of the factors that go into option pricing are volatility and time value. In an extremely turbulent time such as this one, it is easy to understand a sharp increase in option volatility. The real danger, however, comes from elsewhere. Although the time value in the premium seems relatively simple, you must remember that it also affects the forward rate on which the OTC option is based. Therefore, when interest rates are jumping around as they were after the lira devaluation and the sterling suspension from the ERM in September 1992, it may be nearly impossible to get a real price on the option from a bank. During this type of market, both traders and dealers find it extremely difficult to hedge a position and control risk. Thus, although the OTC option market is very liquid, some caution must be used when taking positions.

Another way to trade cross rates on an exchange is through warrants. Traditionally reserved for conservative investors in the stock market, warrants long served as fringe securities usually found as part of a package deal of debt and equity instruments. New life was breathed into the warrants market in the late 1980s, however, as warrants on foreign exchanges became popular. One stock investor—too conservative to play futures markets—told us how he went out on a limb back in 1988 after reading an article in *The Wall Street Journal* about currency warrants trading in Toronto Stock Exchange (before they were finally accepted by the SEC in the United States and traded on the American Stock Exchange in New York). He purchased two yen puts for $300 apiece over the protests of his seasoned broker, who had suggested Australian money markets instead. After the puts doubled their value in six months while the Aussie certificates laid stagnant, the broker began calling other customers and initiated a significant amount of business in the currency warrants markets. Within weeks these warrants were a regular feature in *The Wall Street Journal*. Unfortunately, only a few warrants exist for the cross-currency speculator.

TRADING CROSS RATES USING THE FUTURES MARKET

Of all the markets previously described, futures are probably the most viable exchange-traded instrument for cross-rate players. They pose a problem, however, because there are two ways of playing a cross rate: using futures on the cross rates themselves or trading a combination of the traditional, non-cross-rate currency futures. To take a position in the former is as easy as putting on a soybean trade. The problem is lack of liquidity, still a major difficulty at least for the Chicago Merc's cross-rate products. Accordingly, many futures traders prefer to use the existing contracts in the yen, D-mark, Swiss, pound, and the Canadian and Aussie dollars, where there is more liquidity. Unfortunately, this is not a simple matter. As will be explained later in the chapter, a cross-rate trade in the futures must be struck by trading only a ratio of futures contracts, not a one-to-one spread. The marketing literature from the Merc at the initiation of the cross-rates contracts heralded the end of the need to engage in ratio spreading and legging in and out of such spreads. These were welcome developments, but the liquidity needs to improve so that large participants can get reasonable executions.

Proponents of either market—exchange-traded derivatives or the cash market—can recite laundry lists of their respective attributes. The following factors favor the futures and options camp, but it is unfair to try to compare these with attributes of the cash market because each market is unique. Two advantages often cited by futures traders are probably the most persuasive. First, whatever the futures market may lack in liquidity it makes up for in accessibility. Not only is it easier to set up an account and begin trading, but the marketplace is theoretically a pool of players of all sizes, designed for the quick fill.

Second, in this regulated marketplace where traders rely on a clearing house as a go-between, players simultaneously have the comfort of knowing there will always be a clearing house on the other side of their trade while also enjoying anonymity. Those dissatisfied with their fill almost always can check time and sales data to see if the fill should have indeed occurred. Also, the spread between the bid and the ask in the particular pit or market usually appears to be the same across all sizes of players, something not true for the cash market.

Some futures brokers also insist the exchanges offer a greater array of types of orders for entering and exiting market. This is a falsehood. Today, banks in the cash market, in addition to limit orders and stop orders, allow nearly any type of entry or exit order the futures exchanges allow. They even have some the exchanges don't have, such as orders contingent on other market fluctuations. For instance, a trader might want to buy a European currency against the yen. Analysis shows that the strongest European currency should be the Swiss franc, but the trader feels that the mark-yen is a more reliable cross rate for technical analysis. In such a situation, the trader could place an order to buy the Swiss-yen when the mark-yen breaks out above a certain level. A bank desk would gladly accept this type of order from a good customer.

Futures on cross rates are relatively new, but even without them traders could still, with some difficulties, trade the cross rates by using dollar based futures contracts. Take the mark-yen rate for example. Assume that June D-mark futures trade 0.6670 $/DM and June yen futures trade 0.7575 $/100 yen, and no mark-yen cross rate contract exists. The *spread* between them is 905 IMM points (where each point equals $12.50). Traders could determine the cross rate by calculating the *ratio* between the two, D-mark futures price divided by yen futures price, which here would yield 0.8805 100 yen/DM (roughly 88 yen to buy one D-mark). The spread does not reflect the cross rate, that is, the direct exchange rate, between the two currencies. Figure 2–5 displays a daily plot of the arithmetic difference, or "spread," between front-month mark and yen futures (light line) versus the ratio of these contract prices (dark line). Figure 2–6 shows the movement of the U.S. Dollar Index futures contract over the same period. The difference between the two lines shown in Figure 2–5 is the difference between the ratio of prices, which should approximate the mark-yen cross rate, and the spread. These figures illustrate the impact the dollar has on the spread. The longer the observed time, the greater the difference between the spread and ratio. In other words, suppose you correctly spotted the start of a major bearish trend in D-mark against the yen, but sold the spread instead of the cross rate. The trade may go your way for some time, but it has the potential to actually lose money, even if you were right on the direction of the cross rate. This is because the movement in the dollar may keep the spread unduly narrow.

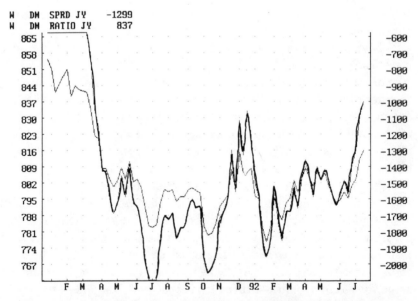

Figure 2–5   Dollar-Mark, Weekly, Spread and Ratio. Light line: Weekly dollar-mark spread, January 1991 to July 1992. Heavy line: Weekly dollar-mark ratio, January 1991 to July 1992. The scale on the left is for the ratio; the scale on the right is for the spread. (*Source:* FutureSource)

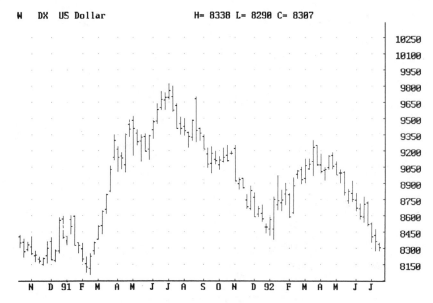

W   DX   US Dollar   H= 8338 L= 8290 C= 8307

Figure 2–6   U.S. Dollar Index, Cash Price from January 1991 to July 1992. (*Source:* FutureSource)

The spread is far from approximation of the cross rate. The reason for the difference in the lines on Figure 2–5 is that the spread still trades the U.S. dollar. Taking a long position in this cross rate by trading the underlying futures contract can be implemented by calculating the correct number of futures contracts to buy and sell. This can be calculated by using the hedge ratio. The formula for this ratio is shown in Figure 2–7.

Attempting to trade cross rates using only conventional, dollar-based futures contracts is no simple matter. In addition to calculating the hedge ratio, the number of contracts must be adjusted to maintain the cross rate ratio as time passes. And if this seems cumbersome, just try putting on an option position using conventional, dollar-based options contracts. The development of cross-rate futures and options has long been needed. Unfortunately, one reason for futures traders to shy away from cross rates, or for cross-rate traders to shy away from futures, may be obvious from the preceding explanation: At present, few liquid futures or options contracts on cross rates exist. As for those that do exist, their volume figures are humbling.

In order to position the futures to most closely track a particular cross rate, the "hedge ratio" - the proportion of buy/sell of one contract versus sell/buy of another - must be determined:

Hedge ratio = $\dfrac{\text{Currency \#1's point value}}{\text{Currency \#2's point value}}$ x   Cross rate

Cross rate = $\dfrac{\text{Value of currency \#1} \quad \text{in US \$}}{\text{Value of currency \#2} \quad \text{in US \$}}$

BP/DM (Sterling-mark) example:

Hedge ratio = $\dfrac{\$6.25/\text{point}\ (\text{pound})}{\$12.50/\text{point}}$ x   2.95 = 1.48

(Three pound futures for each two D-mark future.)

DM/JY (Mark-yen) example:

Hedge ratio = $\dfrac{\$12.50/\text{point}\ (\text{mark})}{\$12.50/\text{point}}$ x   0.91 = 0.91

(Nine D-Mark futures for each group of ten Swiss futures.)

Figure 2–7   Formulas and Examples of Calculation of Hedge Ratio to Determine Number of Futures Contracts Needed to Approximate True Cross Rate.

THE INTERBANK MARKET: AN OVERVIEW

Over the past few years, many investment advisors and futures traders have discovered a hidden gem. The interbank market is open all night, the average trade equals about 20 futures contracts, the expiration date and size of the contract are custom-made, roughly four times as many exchange rates are traded, and your broker often takes the opposite side of the trade. Quite a change of pace for the futures or options trader.

Being open all night also often means many sleepless ones for interbank traders. The following show global times corresponding to New York's noon (E.S.T.):

New York	London	Frankfurt	Singapore	Tokyo	Sydney
Noon	5 P.M.	6 P.M.	Midnight	1 A.M.	2 A.M.

A variety of trading vehicles also exist in the interbank market. A trader can choose among forward, spot, or over-the-counter option transactions. Currency swaps have also grabbed some of the limelight in recent years, although their use is more prevalent among banks and large commercial companies than among speculators. The most popular currency futures contracts have stolen little volume away from these markets, and the arrival of cross-rate futures has largely gone without notice. Far and away, the most popular interbank instrument for speculators is the forward contract perhaps, ironically, because it most resembles a futures contract. Like a futures contract, a forward contract is a contract to buy or sell a quantity of foreign currency at a certain exchange rate at a certain date in the future. Any of the terms of the forward contract are negotiable. For example, a trader could buy mark-yen for delivery in two weeks, instead of the exchange-specified date. Futures contracts, on the other hand, are geared for fungibility: contracts of set amounts and with set delivery dates, where the only thing that's negotiable is price. In the bank forward market, the trader decides both delivery date and amount. Traders with experience in bank forwards from the agricultural markets are probably just starting to yawn at this point. But don't skip ahead—what goes into pricing a forward contract in currency at your local bank is quite different from that involved in contracting out the price for a bushel of wheat or barrel of crude.

In the same way that the Chicago Merc uses its traditional currency futures to price the expiration value of its cross rate futures, cross rate forwards for U.S. banks are usually contracts based on two other foreign exchange forwards, with some special twists. The trader's bank usually incorporates the costs of its doing business—and whatever other profits it can garner—into the price of the forward contract. The bank will make its price in the form of spread. This spread is usually much less than it would charge for spot transactions and usually widens with the length of the forward contract. Typically the spread on a dollar-based, one week forward will be about $1/10$ of a pip, the term used to describe one point in the cash market, and a three-month forward will be about 2 pips. This rate will vary with market conditions. Banks usually are able to offer tighter spreads on forwards because they have already made their money on the spot transaction. The forward transaction usually starts out as a spot transaction, and then the trader rolls a position forward to a date of his choice. This is true of either dollar-based forwards or cross-currency forwards. Pricing is a function of time and liquidity in the forward markets, and the major crosses are extremely liquid. Banks actively quote a wide range of forward prices on all the major currencies. In Figure 2–8 notice how these prices are quoted as a bid/ask just like the spot prices. According to Figure 2–8, for example, a trader who wants to buy a 6-month forward in Dollar-Mark can do so by buying dollars at 1.5236, which is the spot price, and then rolling this position out 6 months, when he would pay the bid on 6-month marks of 446. This means the final forward rate would be 1.5236 + .0446, or 1.5682. If the trader were selling dollars, he would subtract the offer of .0445 from the spot price.

Although forwards are the instrument of choice as of this writing, capital requirement rules are bringing in a new one, forward rate agreements (FRAs). A forward rate agreement is a contract between two parties who agree to deposit an interest rate for a fixed period of time, beginning sometime in the future. Another way of explaining an

COMPOSITE SPOT/FORWARD RATES

GLD	AD/AUS DOLLAR		BF/BELGIAN FR		BP/PND STG		CD/CAN DOLLAR		DG/DUTCH	
SP	.7477	2	31.337	80	1.9040	2	1.1964	82	1.7170	9
1M	15	17	146	162	104	95	19	9	85	89
2M	27	30	289	315	198	189	33	24	168	172
3M	38	41	460	460	291	281	46	35	248	252
6M	63	70	856	910	560	549	89	84	483	487
1Y	100	115	1545	1650	1006	988	159	155	870	886

	DK/DAN KR		DM/D. MARK		EC/ECU		FM/FIN MKKA		FR/FRENCH FR	
SP	5.8555	614	1.5230	6	1.3450	45	4.1490	540	5.1275	95
1M	343	371	78	78	78	79	330	360	328	238
2M	640	699	153	153	153	153	655	705	588	502
3M	941	1006	227	227	224	225	985	1055	854	767
6M	1777	1911	445	446	434	434	2020	2170	1621	1545
1Y	3296	3479	797	812	771	768	3760	4010	2882	2835

	HD/HK DOLLAR		IL/ITL LIRA		IP/IRISH PD		JY/YEN		ND/NZ DOLLAR	
SP	7.7289	300	1151.0	20	1.7486	55	125.75	80	.5448	53
1M	40	20	101	106	91	98	8	9	23	29
2M	65	40	187	195	175	186	14	15	22	40
3M	80	50	274	283	260	277	19	20	33	51
6M	81	50	540	553	509	526	19	20	57	60
1Y	23	125	992	1023	899	941	5		100	103

	NK/NOR KR		SD/SING DOLLAR		SF/SWISS FR		SK/SWED KR		SP/SPAN PTA	
SP	5.9648	75	1.6167	90	1.3728	45	5.5025	75	96.080	125
1M	312	340	16	5	64	55	345	370	670	745
2M	625	675	26	5	125	117	677	725	1324	1445
3M	931	985	36		186	178	1014	1070	2026	2132
6M	1816	1940	56		352	347	2038	2150	4140	4305
1Y	3334	3550	81	20	605	602	3833	4025	7830	8055

Figure 2–8 Various Currencies Spot and Forward Rates. Listed in order of spot, 1 month, 2 months, 3 months, 6 months and 1 year. (*Source:* Bloomberg L.P.)

FRA is that if a trader wants to borrow money in a certain currency for a period of time, say 3 months, and lend it for another period of time, say 6 months, he can buy a 3-month 6-month FRA. In other words, he is trading the spread between 3-month rates and 6-month rates. However, unlike a cash transaction, the principal amount does not change hands. Instead, settlement is made of the interest rate differential at the expiration of the shorter dated side of the agreement, or 3 months in the preceding example. FRAs offer a very liquid way to lock in a future interest rate in any actively traded currency or cross rate. If this sounds a lot like a calendar spread in, say, Euromark futures, that's exactly what it is. The difference is that the FRA provides more liquidity and flexibility because the trader can have the contract for any desired interest period. Furthermore, banks are using FRAs more and more because no principal changes hands, so assets are not being used.

As stated earlier, the interbank market comprises much more than banks alone. Essentially, there are four types of players, not counting the actual hedger or speculators: (1) large banks; (2) broker-dealers; (3) central banks of various countries; (4) large multinational corporations with active foreign currency operations. The majority of transactions, except for speculative ones taken by broker-dealers, are initiated by a bank in one of two ways: Either the bank trades directly with another bank, or the bank trades through a broker-dealer. In the 1980s, the trend appeared to be going more toward the latter type.

In any case, banks can make markets in several ways. If they are quoting a price to a client, they will generally make a two-way market. The client will ask for a price on a specific currency for a specific size, but not reveal the direction of the trade. The bank dealer will then quote a price, giving both the bid and offer. This spread is generally 5 to 10 pips, or cash points, but may vary depending on size or the liquidity in the market. The client may then buy at the offer or sell at the bid, and may also ask the bank trader to try to execute at a different price. For example, if mark-yen is offered at 82.50, the trader may put in an order to buy it below the market at 82.40. If the mark-yen is later offered at 82.40, the order will be filled. This is similar to a "limit" or "or better" order in the futures market. A trader may also ask for a price in a currency and tell the bank dealer which way she wants to go, buy or sell. Sometimes bank dealers will give a better price in this situation than when responding to a two-way price request. This is because they will not have to price their markup onto both the bid and offer, and because they know which way they will need to trade to offset the position.

Banks deal very actively with each other, often through a computerized system known as direct dealing. Participating banks may request a price from another bank by just typing the currency and size of the trade into a computer. The other bank will put its price onto the computer, and the asking bank can trade at that price merely by hitting a button on the computer. This type of trading is very common and makes up a significant portion of daily trading volume at foreign exchange banks.

Foreign exchange banks also may trade through brokers. Typically, this trade goes both ways—the bank can get prices from the broker, or vice versa. These trades are usually done by voice through a "box" in which the banks can hear the broker-dealer quotes. The broker is constantly giving a bid and offer price. The size of the quote depends on the broker's relationship with the bank. As an example, a typical upper-tier bank would know that any price being quoted would be good for $5 million. The broker might under some circumstances, such as extreme volatility or periods of low liquidity, qualify a bid or offer to a smaller size. Of course the broker may also have a much larger amount than $5 million to buy or sell, so the bank dealer must be careful. For instance, if the dealer were to say "mine, everything," indicating an intent to buy all the broker had to sell, the response, "yours, $200 million," would mean the dealer had just bought $200 million dollars of currency. This broker market is also viewed as being the most current market available, and is the first to move. It is much quicker than the screens in the banks. In fact, most currency traders have heard the phrase "You can't trust your screens" to obtain current prices. In other words, if the market is moving fast, you may not be able to trade at the price on the quote screen.

In addition to currency brokers, a bank may call a traditional futures wire house for pricing, or the house may call the bank. Typically, this type of trade is treated as customer business by the bank. The better the relationship between the wire house and the bank, the tighter the bid-ask spreads and the more aggressive the pricing.

Finally, most banks will quote major cross rates to customers. However, many banks will not quote, or at least not actively quote, exotic cross rates. For example, a U.S. bank may not actively quote a cross rate such as the sterling-ringgit. A trader who needed a fast quote to trade this cross would most likely need to call a bank in either Malaysia or London, England, which is a major money center. Typically, traders should call a bank in one of the underlying countries for an exotic cross rate. Traders lacking a relationship with a bank in either country may instruct their own bank to deal on their behalf. This can be both cumbersome and expensive. The ideal way to execute a transaction such as this is to set up a relationship with the foreign bank before the transaction is made.

Why are banks so willing to quote cross rates? Simply stated, the market in forwards largely exists to serve businesses that will require some foreign currency at some future date. If it is mid-February when a Canadian business learns it will need to make a DM 10,000 payment to a German supplier in mid-June, the company can do several things to secure the currency for the payment. Keep in mind that the cross rate between the C-dollar and the D-mark can change a great deal in the four-month period. The least risky option is for the Canadian firm to purchase the D-marks *forward* by four months: Buy the D-marks in February to receive them in June. On the other hand, the firm could simply buy *spot* D-marks in June. "Spot" foreign exchange is often used interchangeably with "cash" since the buyer obtains the currency now. In truth, because the currency takes two days to deliver, a spot transaction could be described as an extremely short-dated forward contract—the bank pays the currency to the buyer's account at a price that may no longer actually be trading at that time. For the Canadian firm, however, buying the marks spot when needed in June might expose the company to higher prices that could have been avoided. Another alternative, buying-and-holding D-marks from February on, might bring about the same result as a forward but would be accompanied by the inconveniences of getting together the cash in a short period of time and possibly establishing a foreign bank account.

For speculators, the maturity of the forward contract in which they take position in the interbank market depends on how long they want to keep the position. The customary time span for most trades varies between one week and three months. Traders with a position lasting longer than that simply keep rolling it over. Two things govern the maturity of traders' forward contracts: how long they plan to maintain the position and how much counterparty risk they are willing to take. As we will discuss later, the pricing of forwards is a direct result of interest rate differentials between the currencies. As interest rates change, the forward rates will also change. From a mathematical viewpoint, it is possible to profit from these changes, and that is exactly what swap traders do. Regardless, most traders using forwards will value them somewhere close to when they think they will be exiting the position. The most commonly quoted forward rate by various financial publications is the 3-month forward, in keeping with the quarterly cycle and with a oft-quoted span of debt instruments. However, as the credit quality of the counterparty becomes a more and more important consideration, maturities of forwards will tend to shorten.

This is a good place to examine some of the issues surrounding the counterparty risk that a trader incurs; that is, the risk that the entity taking the other side of the trade will default before the forward contract matures. The best way to understand counterparty risk is by looking at an example of a trade. Let's say that a trader buys $50 million of mark-yen from a bank and has the forward contract dated at three months. The bank then goes out of business and defaults on its obligations during that three-month period. The funds held at the bank are most likely in some sort of security for margin purposes and are probably not lost in the default. However, any open profit on the trade is a liability of the bank and would probably be lost. One way to lessen this risk is to keep maturities of forward contracts short and thus reduce the time that the potential liability is possible. Another reason counterparty failure is dangerous is that a failure in one major bank could spread to others because they all have credit facilities and trading lines with each other.

Once a position has been established in the cash market, most traders convert it into a forward. In a forward contract transaction, the bank acts as principal. It officially acts as the other side of the trade. Once a position in a forward contract is on, it is not offset in the same fashion as a futures contract. A forward contract can be offset in two ways: either with another forward transaction or with a spot transaction. The forward transaction would entail doing a spot transaction in the opposite direction of the original trade, in the same amount as the original trade, and then rolling it out to the correct value date by using a swap. This would directly offset the original transaction, and there would no longer be any price or interest rate risk. However, the profit or loss on the trade could not be taken out of the account until the value date of the position, since there are technically still two positions on. On the other hand, the trader may offset a forward contract with a spot transaction by executing a trade in the cash market in the opposite direction of the original trade, but not rolling it forward. This process takes the price risk out of the position but the interest rate risk still remains because the trader will need to roll the position one day at a time until the value date, or physically take or make delivery of the currency. As interest rate differentials change before the value date is reached, the cost of the roll will also change. Thus there is some interest rate risk involved. For this reason, as well as the cost of rolling on a daily basis, nearly all forward contract offset trades are also done as forwards.

A novice to the interbank market may quickly devise some grand schemes playing on the relationship between spot and forward transactions. Among all this talk of cross rates, one that may come to mind is taking advantage of discrepancies between the cross rate and its dollar-based component currencies. This is what the market calls "triangular arbitrage." Like a similar ploy touched on earlier when discussing cross-rate trades in the futures markets, two exchange rates always imply a third rate. Say, for instance—taking the middle ground between the bid and the ask—dollar-mark is trading 1.6510 DM/$ while dollar-yen goes for 150.10 yen/$. These two rates imply a mark-yen rate of 90.91 JY/DM. If any of the three rates in this exchange rate triangle are out of line, an arbitrage opportunity would exist. Therefore, if the mark-yen cross rate, for instance, was found trading for 98.50 JY/DM while the other two rates remained the same, a trader could effectively buy 200,000 D-marks for $121,140, then sell the 200,000 marks for 19,700,000 yen. The trader would quickly use the 19,700,000 yen to purchase $131,240, thus netting $10,100 on the whole deal, not counting transaction costs. Such plays were actually possible for banks several years ago when the foreign exchange market was much less developed. Today, the markets are very liquid and efficient, and any discrepancies between spot and forward rates are immediately traded out of the market. Such arbitrage plays are rare and usually achieved only by traders sitting on a bank desk specializing in this type of transaction. By the time other traders, even very large sophisticated ones, see the opportunity, it is gone.

CROSSING OVER TO THE INTERBANK MARKET

With all deference toward the futures exchanges, the bottom line is that the best place for the serious cross-rate trader is the interbank market. The following should touch on most of the major considerations facing new traders in this vast market.

One of the primary considerations in using the interbank market is margining. Banks allow traders to trade forwards via lines of credit or a version of margin arrangement. Credit lines work like a credit agreement or a noncollateralized loan. The trader deposits an agreed amount in the bank, allowing him to deal in forward contracts, and the bank takes the risk of any devastating moves in the foreign exchange markets. Credit lines vary between 5 and 20 times the deposited funds. In other words, if the customer deposits $1 million, the bank will give him authority to trade a position of up to $5 to $20 million. Exactly where in this range the customer falls depends on what type of customer he is, his existing relationship with the bank, his experience and reputation, and the aggressiveness of the bank. Commodity trading advisors (CTAs) entering the interbank market are typically allowed a leverage factor of 15 to 20 times capital, the latter corresponding to roughly 5% margin, slightly higher than that demanded in most futures-trading accounts of the same size. The interbank market also usually demands a maintenance margin requirement. This operates much like it does in the futures brokerages, where additional funds must be deposited or positions closed out if the value of the account drops to below a set level. This level varies from bank to bank, but usually ranges from 25% to 50%.

So once a customer deposits funds at a foreign exchange-trading bank and negotiates a credit line, he can begin trading. There are other ways to accomplish this, for many traders do not actually need to deposit funds in order to transact business. Two alternatives readily come to mind. First, when the customer is already a client of the bank, as is the case with many corporate clients, the relationship already in place may suffice. For instance, suppose that General Motors carried out its corporate banking activities with a certain bank. There would be billions of dollars flowing through and being held by that bank each year. Because of this relationship, GM could trade foreign exchange without posting any money in a separate account for that purpose. The existing banking relationship would allow GM to trade, and the firm would be granted a trading limit, called a line, based on its corporate balance sheet. This constitutes the most common type of trading arrangement in the foreign exchange markets.

Another means of trading without actually depositing funds is to obtain a letter of credit (LC). A letter of credit is a promise, usually issued by a bank on behalf of one of its clients, to accept a transaction. For those unfamiliar with LCs, they work as follows: A client obtains an LC from her personal bank for $1 million and pays a yearly service charge; she then takes it to a trading bank and opens a foreign exchange transaction account. If her trading is profitable, her account at the trading bank will be credited with the profits. If she loses money, then the trading bank will ask her personal bank for funds. The customer will then have a debt to her personal bank, on which she must pay interest. Obviously, this is a highly leveraged way to trade. A trader with a $1 million LC may be allowed to trade up to $20 million worth of currencies and, if the trading is successful, never have to put up a dime. In such a situation, the leverage is infinite in a sense; however, the flip side is infinite loss. Traders may also lose money that they have not posted and are actually borrowing to trade. Although this is a very risky way to trade in the currency markets, it gives the cash foreign exchange markets a distinct advantage over the futures markets.

Another question is which currency to use for the excess funds in the account. For U.S.-based traders, an often overlooked yet important aspect of trading currencies through a bank account is the option to denominate that account in a currency other than U.S. dollars. The concept of denominating the account in another currency is a perfectly normal one to non-U.S. players. Any bank trading foreign exchange will convert the funds on deposit into any liquid currency, and hold the deposit in that form until otherwise instructed. So why would someone want to hold deposits in another currency? Because of two possible advantages: interest rate and currency appreciation. First, at this writing, the U.S. dollar is at a huge interest rate disadvantage to the European currencies. Dollar-based interest rates are currently around 3.75%, while German rates float around 9.5%. Since D-mark deposits automatically earn D-mark interest rates, it is advantageous to hold funds in D-marks instead of dollars. A trader could also choose another currency with even higher rates.

The danger in this approach lies in the possibility that the currency may move relative to the dollar. For example, if a U.S.-based trader held his deposit in D-marks, he may be able to pick up almost 6.0% in interest rate differential. However, this gain could be lost if the dollar were to rise by more than 6.0%. This is why long-term rather than short-term traders employ this strategy. A trader with a one-year time horizon in the preceding example enjoys a 6.0% cushion to work with. However, a trader with a one-month horizon has much less to gain by choosing an alternative currency. The interest rate advantage of a D-mark account breaks down to 0.5% a month. It would take a price movement from 1.7000 to 1.7085 to eradicate this gain, and a move of this size is a daily occurrence. Therefore, short-term traders generally should not consider denominating their account in a non-home currency.

One alternative is to hold both a long- and short-term view. For instance, a trader may believe that the best currency from a price perspective over the next year is the Swiss franc. Since the Swiss has become a high-yielding currency, the trader could deposit the funds to earn both the positive interest rate differential and the price appreciation. He would then trade his short-term signals, but leave his excess funds in Swiss francs. This technique appears to be commonly used among many market participants.

The measurement of profits and losses is a major hurdle for traders in the futures market who want to begin trading in the cash cross rate market. Numerous differences in accounting for profits exist between the interbank and futures markets. Cross rates add some more twists.

First, the cash market requires an understanding of "unmatured" profit and loss. Since the trader and the counterparty, usually a bank, set the value date of the forward contract at the initiation of the trade, the trade may be closed out before that value date. If this happens, there is a profit or loss on the trade, but it is not officially closed out until the value date comes. The question is then whether to treat an unmatured profit or loss as open trade equity, or realized profit or loss, at month's end. Most traders handle this dilemma in one of two ways: They either treat an unmatured but closed-out position at the end of the month as realized profit or loss, or set up the forward contract to expire on the last day of the month. The first approach offers much more flexibility, but the latter is a simpler and more practical alternative.

Other twists that are added by trading cross rates in the cash foreign exchange market are caused by the settlement of the position in a currency other than U.S. dollars. For example, a trader who bought the mark-yen cross at 78.50 and sold it later at 79.50 would have profit of 1.00. But what currency is the profit in? While the cross rate essentially prices the D-mark, the profit is in yen. In other words, if the size of the position was DM 10 million, the trader would be liquidating that DM 10 million for yen, this time getting JY 795 million back. The trader is left with a residue of foreign currency that is profit.

Quoting the mark-yen cross in this fashion—number of yen it takes to make up one D-mark—is the market convention. If truly desired, a trader could get the bank to quote "yen-mark," that is, the cross rate in terms of D-marks, not yen, although this is rarely done. The convention for other cross rates is that profits in sterling-mark are measured in marks, profits in mark-Swiss are measured in Swiss francs, profits in sterling-yen in yen, and so on. As stated earlier, exchange rates for the U.S. dollar can also be considered cross rates. Here, however, banks will readily quote in either dollar amounts or foreign currency amounts. If foreign currency amounts are used, the profit will be in dollars; if the trader goes by dollar amounts, the profit will be in the currency. For example, a trader who says "buy 50 dollars of dollar-mark at 155.25" is buying $50 million dollars worth, though the profit or loss will be measured in D-marks. On the other hand, a trader who says "buy 50 marks at 155.25" is trading foreign currency amounts, and the profit or loss will be in U.S. dollars.

In the trading of cross rates, not dollars, profits and losses that accrue in other currencies pose several questions. First, how do traders convert these profits or losses back to their home currency (here, dollars), and second, is further currency risk involved? Converting back into dollars is simple enough; if there is a profit in the account of DM 1 million, they can be sold for dollars and the account becomes a dollar-balance account. If the D-marks are held for awhile, however, currency risk comes into play, though it is slight compared to the risk of the cross-rate position. The following table shows relative currency prices for a hypothetical trade.

	Entry	Exit
D-mark	1.6050	1.5500
S-franc	1.4075	1.4075
Mark-Swiss	87.690	90.810

Profit 3.120 S-francs

Were this trade realized, the profit could then be converted to dollars by selling the 3.120 francs at the going rate of 1.4075. There is a small price risk in doing this since even if the S-franc were to move by 1%, it would only change the profit by 0.0312 S-francs. The point is that the money is made or lost trading cross rates on the cross itself, not on converting that profit or loss back into dollars.

Another concern for traders of cross rates, especially commodity trading advisors, is record keeping. As recently as 1990, many banks did not provide customers with daily recaps of trades and open positions, or monthly statements. The only documentation of a trade was a confirmation of the trade. This was standard practice and generally was acceptable for most traditional bank foreign exchange customers. However, in the past few years, as more CTAs and investment advisors have started using the cash markets, the banks have responded to their needs by providing much better daily and monthly statements.

Unlike the futures industry, the interbank market has no clearing corporation. Unless otherwise contracted with the bank, traders must be prepared to perform themselves many typical "back office" functions of the clearing house or broker in the securities and futures industries. Marking positions to market becomes increasingly difficult along with the number and variety of instruments. The combination of forwards, cash, and OTC options can be cumbersome to value on an intraday basis.

Trade accounting for traders carrying positions for others is another matter. Most trading advisors with experience in the futures or securities markets make use of some sort of accounting package anyway. Most, but not all, of these systems are sophisticated enough to handle cash foreign exchange, non-dollar-denominated assets and OTC options. For successful trading advisors, keeping a well-maintained back office or administrative department is a must. Many trading managers feel that the most critical part of their business is a smooth flowing back office—an interesting sentiment considering their main business function is trading.

Not only do banks make up the market, they serve as the trader's broker-dealer. A trader should try to establish a relationship with a bank that understands the trader's needs, that is, one with desk traders willing to talk (for "seat-of-the-pants" traders), or one that quickly gets the trader in the market and shuts up (for trading advisors). Some larger traders have noticed better results with trading volume spread evenly across a number of banks, while others do all their business with one source. Most traders find that all large foreign exchange bank desks will give comparable pricing. Therefore, traders may find it helpful to develop a relationship with one or more banks where they will feel comfortable giving the bank trader a small amount of discretion in filling the order. This type of order is usually placed as an "at best" order or entered with a limit. For example, a trader may instruct the bank trader, "Buy 50 dollars of dollar-mark at best." This means that the bank trader should buy $50 million of marks at the best price then available. This order is similar to a market order in the futures market. The trader may also place an order by saying, "Buy 50 dollars of dollar-mark, work it, but don't pay more than 1.6050." This means the trader wants to buy $50 million of D-marks but is giving the bank trader discretion on the price, as long as it doesn't exceed 1.6050. Sometimes time constraints will also be placed on an order. These orders are usually best suited for quiet markets. If the market is moving away quickly, the trader should trade at the current bid or offer. Placing limit orders can save three to five pips on a trade but may cost much more if the order is not filled in a fast-moving market.

Another important consideration in choosing a bank is trading size. Most large money-center banks will rarely even look at someone managing less than $1 million to $2 million. Some banks are starting to solicit traders with accounts ranging from $400,000 to $800,000, on the condition, however, that the trader trades frequently and in large amounts. Some others have expressed willingness to go even lower, provided they can be assured the trader's account size will grow.

Several cautions exist for the futures trader now entering the interbank foreign exchange market to trade cross rates. One crucial point is terminology. Suppose you have spent months trading in one of the IMM futures markets, the D-mark for instance. Despite all the action in that market, you decide to enter the interbank market. You meet all the criteria discussed earlier for entering the cash realm, you've opened an account at a reliable bank, and you are about to make your first trade. Not terribly concerned with trade location, you tell the dealer simply to buy the market on close. Hopefully, common sense will intervene before the dealer has to inform you that in a 24-hour market there is no "close." Later, as the bank's market in D-marks is trading 1.6260–1.6265, you want to get in quickly so you instruct your broker to buy $800,000 worth of D-marks at the bank's offer of 1.6265. The dealer will be instantly confused, because 1.6265 is where the bank wants to buy D-marks, not sell them. The lower number in the interbank market is usually the offer for the currency. The bank is quoting prices to buy or sell dollars; hence the confusion of being able to buy at the bid or sell at the offer. Some markets, however, are by custom quoted in currency, similar to the futures markets. The most active of these is the British pound, but they also include the Australian dollar and Irish pound.

An example of a real-life conversation between an interbank customer and the bank dealer might proceed in the following manner, assuming the dollar-mark is trading near 1.6275 DM/$: The customer calls and asks what the market is in dollar-mark (dollars priced in D-marks) for five dollars ($5 million); the desk trader answers "75–80." This means that D-marks can be purchased with dollars for 1.6275 DM/$ or sold at 1.6280 DM/$, considering the quantity of $5 million. The conversation goes much the same way even when a cross rate is being quoted. There is little use in the customer trying to double-check the pricing of the cross rate quote using two dollar-based transactions, for not only is the market's efficiency such that it will work out the exact same way, but even if there were an arbitrage opportunity, the market would move by the time the trader pushes the "equals" button on a calculator.

THE FUTURE DEVELOPMENT OF INTERBANK AND EXCHANGE-TRADED MARKETS

Futures contracts for currencies exist almost entirely in the United States. These markets are mostly dollar-based contracts, which have enjoyed a healthy chunk of trading volume of dollars versus D-marks, yen, Swiss francs, British pounds, Aussie dollars, and Canadian dollars. Cross-rate futures, sadly enough, have not made much progress at this writing. Nonetheless, there is something that may breathe new life into cross rate futures trading, and its name is Globex. The agreement between the Chicago Merc and Reuters Information Service calls for an electronic after-hours exchange for various exchange-traded financial products. Trading in D-mark and yen futures and options officially commenced in late June 1992, and other futures and options are scheduled to be added during the ensuing months.

Initially, the Merc and Board of Trade as well as the MATIF in Paris will participate by listing some of their products. It is hoped that other exchanges will come on board as time passes, and that at some future point in time most, if not all, futures contracts will be traded around the clock. When Globex appears to be trading at full steam and with sufficient volume, it will provide an excellent forum for trading cross-rate futures on a 24-hour basis. For North Americans at least, until Globex, the existing cross-rate futures contracts have not exactly been a recipe for success. Having the most international of exchange rates traded only during IMM trading hours did not cause traders to beat a global path to the Merc's door. Opening these rates up to a 24-hour arena through Globex may be a solution.

Globex will work by electronically matching orders of member firms. It will automatically match a market order to buy with the lowest offer on the system and will provide an excellent audit trail of all trades. The system is set up to run only during hours when the exchanges are closed, so it is an exchange enhancement rather than a competing product. As of this writing, Globex is in its formative stages, and only time will tell if it can be a success.

Many cash traders don't understand what the furor of trading futures on nonexchange hours is all about. They have been doing it in the metals and currency markets for years by using an instrument called an Exchange for Physical, or EFP. An EFP is a way of exchanging a position in the cash market for a futures position by using swaps. A simple example can be seen in the cash currency market. Assume that a trader is long 100 contracts of September D-marks, and some sort of news out at 3:00 A.M. in New York makes him want to liquidate this position. If he were limited to trading futures, he would have to wait until 8:20 A.M. to sell his futures out. However, by establishing trading lines, the trader may exit the position via an EFP. Here is how it works. The trader will get a price on 12.5 million marks against the dollar (the equivalent of 100 futures contracts). He will then sell the marks in the spot market. At that time, or in the morning, he can instruct the bank trading desk to "EFP it" to September futures. The bank will calculate the carry charge to the forward date that matches the IMM expiration date for the September contract and add or subtract that from the cash price. This forward contract then exactly matches the contract specifications for a futures contract, and can be treated as one. The bank will then "give up" the EFP to the exchange floor as a futures contract, and the trader has effectively offset a futures position in the middle of the night. A huge amount of EFP business is conducted on a daily basis. Banks are happy to do this business because they make money in several ways. First, there is a spread on the original cash transaction of 5 to 10 pips, or between about $25 and $50 per contract. This should be compared with the spread between the bid and offer on a futures contract, which usually ranges from $12.50 to $25. The bank also may charge for executing the EFP, and this usually amounts to about $2 per contract. The bank also makes money by rounding. When converting the cash position, which may be carried out to five decimal places, to futures, which is carried out to two decimal places, the calculations very seldom come out even. The bank will always round the difference in their favor. If you add up these costs, an EFP can be quite expensive, especially for a cash trader who is accustomed to dealing for almost nothing. However, this cost can be small compared with the loss sustained during a large market move, if a trader is able to exit a position in the middle of the night to protect profits. How many traders will use the facilities provided by Globex and how many will continue to use

EFPs? Only time can answer this question. The exchanges are losing volume to the cash market through EFPs, and some have even restricted their use to instances where there will be physical delivery of the underlying instrument. The Chicago Merc and others may become more aggressive in this regard to protect Globex as it grows. In any case, events should be interesting to watch as Globex develops. Cross-rate futures' past disappointments may become Globex's future gains. However, EFPs have traditionally worked well in markets where a liquid futures and a centrally organized cash market exist, so they may maintain their current status as the instrument of choice.

3

VARIETIES OF CROSS RATES

CURRENCY BLOCS OF THE WORLD

Anyone familiar with the foreign exchange markets knows that certain currencies move together. Some of the discussion in the following section, for instance, deals with the difference in behavior of an exchange-rate between two neighboring countries that are each other's greatest trading partner, versus the activity between two remote countries with very little mutual trade.

When economists talk of currency blocs, they are often fond of discussing both trade and regional factors that play a role in forming the groups. The truth is, currency groups are almost synonymous with trade blocs. The industrialized world is divided into three major trading blocs: the European bloc, the dollar bloc, and the yen bloc. The European bloc could also be called the D-mark bloc since the mark is its dominant currency, and many of the other European currencies are actively quoted in terms of marks. For example, the mark-guilder is much more actively quoted by banks than the dollar-guilder. Behind the mark fall most of the members of the European Community (EC), which now includes Germany, Britain, Greece, Portugal, France, Italy, Holland,

Belgium, Denmark, Ireland, and Spain. Also included in this club are the Nordic currencies such as the Norwegian krone, Swedish krona, and Finnish markka, and of course the Swiss franc and Austrian schilling. To citizens of those countries whose national identity gets offended when their currency is so automatically linked with another, perhaps the term "group" should be better defined. Trading in the same group does not mean the country's central bank follows the Bundesbank with a lemminglike obedience. For example, the exchange rate between Germany and Switzerland has been a veritable roller coaster over the past year (see Figure 3–1). A simple way to detect how a currency is grouped is by comparing two currencies against a currency of another group to see, literally, what their price histories look like. A more sophisticated definition would entail some heavy statistics. Taking the simple approach, a chart of the mark-French and mark-yen can be compared with dollar-mark, dollar-French, and dollar-yen. As can be seen in Figures 3–2 through 3–6, there is a much greater variation in the dollar-based crosses than in the mark-yen and in mark-French. The mark-yen is also characterized by larger moves than are seen in mark-French, because the economies of Germany and France are more closely linked than those of Germany and Japan.

The dollar bloc does not contain as many currencies as the Europe bloc, and most of its members enjoy greater latitude. Ironically many of

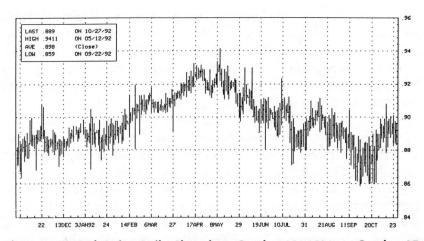

LAST	.889	ON 10/27/92
HIGH	.9411	ON 05/12/92
AVE	.898	(Close)
LOW	.859	ON 09/22/92

Figure 3–1 Mark-Swiss, Daily Chart from October 30, 1991, to October 27, 1992. This is a good example of a cross rate between closely tied trading partners. There is some variation, but the cross rate stays within general boundaries. (*Source:* Bloomberg L.P.)

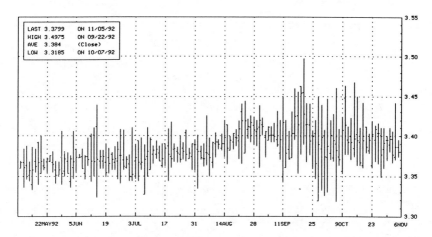

Figure 3–2 Mark-French, Daily Chart from May 11, 1992, to November 5, 1992. This is an example of a cross rate between trading partners in a fixed exchange rate system. (*Source:* Bloomberg L.P.)

these happen to be representatives of the former British Empire including the Canadian dollar; at times, the Australian and New Zealand dollars; and the Hong Kong dollar. On occasion, the "four Asian tiger" countries—South Korea, Taiwan, Malaysia, and Singapore—have actually pegged their currency to the U.S. unit, although the latter two have done this less in recent years.

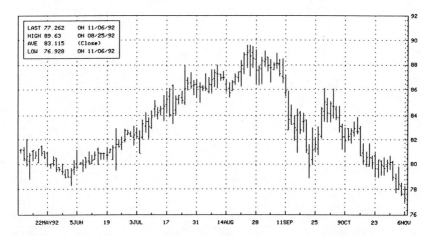

Figure 3–3 Mark-Yen, Daily Chart from May 11, 1992, to November 6, 1992. This is an example of a nondollar cross rate between trading partners. (*Source:* Bloomberg L.P.)

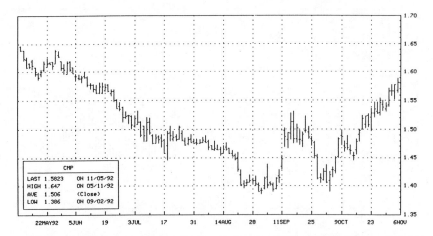

Figure 3–4 Dollar-Mark, Daily Chart from May 5, 1992, to November 5, 1992. This is an example of a dollar-based exchange rate. As of this writing, the dollar-mark is the most actively traded exchange rate in the world. (*Source:* Bloomberg L.P.)

The Japanese yen appears to be a group in itself, an independent, in a way. As one trader once said, "In a market of Ivy Leagues and Big Tens, the Japanese yen is a bit of Notre Dame." No other currency either officially or in practice has linked its value to the yen. That country's efforts to construct an East Asia trading bloc may one day change this.

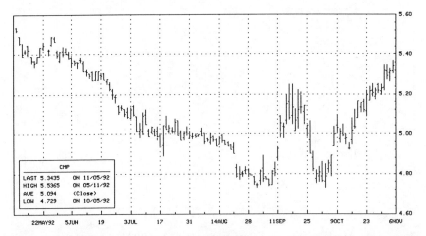

Figure 3–5 Dollar-French, Daily Chart from May 11, 1992, to November 5, 1992. This is an example of an actively traded dollar-based exchange rate. Notice the similarities to dollar-mark. (*Source:* Bloomberg L.P.)

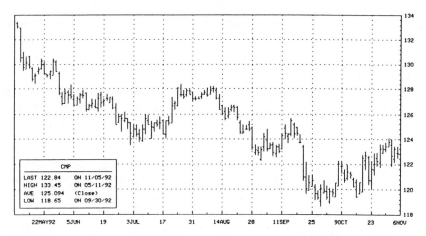

Figure 3–6   Dollar-Yen, Daily Chart from May 11, 1992, to November 5, 1992. This is an example of a dollar-based exchange rate with a non-European currency. (*Source:* Bloomberg L.P.)

Finally, we have the former communist states of Eastern Europe and the once-Soviet lands. Only time will tell whether these states' currencies will form a bloc of their own or follow the rest of Europe in obedience to the D-mark. If the recent developments in Hungary are any sign, it may be the latter.

TYPES OF CROSS RATES

The various cross-rate markets actively traded in the foreign exchange arena can be divided into particular categories. The most obvious groupings would be those rates between trading partners that involve some semifixed exchange rate system such as Europe's Exchange Rate Mechanism (ERM), high-yield versus low-yield cross rates, and exotic cross rates. We will examine each separately.

TRADING PARTNERS

Cross rates between trading partners may be the easiest variety to follow and trade. The major crosses, such as the mark-yen, sterling-mark, and mark-Swiss, involve the relationship between the currencies of countries that have well-established trading relationships. (Two of the most liquid "trading partner" markets in the world are dollar-mark and dollar-yen.) Under such circumstances, the cross rates enjoy natural liquidity and activity due to the assortment of commercial trading relationships already in place.

To trade these markets effectively, a trader must understand the fundamental factors that affect the movement of the cross rates. In the trading partner cross rates, movement depends on economic differences between the countries, including relative rates of inflation, production, monetary policy, capital flows, and many other economic factors. Yet either because of the quickness of the market in interpreting these factors or the sheer volume of trading partner markets, many of the more active examples of these rates—sterling-mark for one—may also be traded profitably by technical trend-following methods. From time to time, these cross rates will trend nicely, but often they can trade in ranges like any commodity. But fundamentals should not be forgotten completely. Reasonable assumptions on the relative strength of the respective economies of two trading partners—an economic, fundamental observation—can provide important clues as to when the cross rate will make a substantial move versus staying in its range. This type of analysis is most easily applied when one economy is overextended in some way. For example, if interest rates in Germany are viewed as being near a high considering the health of the German economy, and strength appears to be gathering in the Japanese economy, the stage may be set for a trend move in the mark-yen cross rate. In other words, the yen may appreciate against the mark because its economy will be faring better.

On the other hand, if there is not real direction in the economic cycles or interest rates, then the cross rate may be confined to a trading range. Trading range markets require a different approach. In a market devoid of any long-term trend, the trader will be successful in buying the low end of the range and selling the high end of the range. The more successful methods for determining when a market is trend mode or trading range mode are discussed at length in Chapter 5. A fine example of these two types of markets can be seen in Figures 3–7 and 3–8. Figure 3–7 shows a nice trading range market in sterling-mark, with highs near 2.95 DM/BP and lows just above 2.80 DM/BP. Figure 3–8 shows the same market over the following several months as sterling-mark trended lower.

Cross-currency rates between trading partner such as the mark-yen are also supported by their respective central banks. This support makes the trading less volatile in the long run since there is incentive to

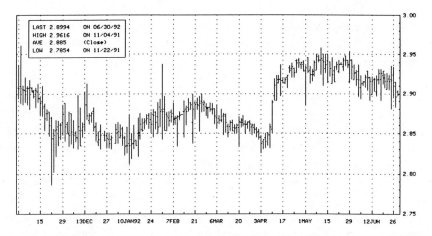

Figure 3–7 Sterling-Mark, Daily Chart from November 1, 1991, to June 30, 1992. This is an example of a trading range market that could have been successfully traded by buying sterling-mark at 2.83 DM/BP, and selling at 2.95 DM/BP. (*Source:* Bloomberg L.P.)

keep the exchange rates stable in order to promote trade between the countries. In contrast, less liquid cross rates, such as ones involving a Middle Eastern currency or Pacific Rim currency, may move a great deal before any controls are put on the move. The problem with trading in this environment is that there may be no bids or offers to liquidate a large open position. Thus, exchange rates between major

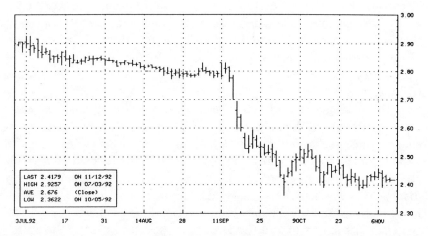

Figure 3–8 Sterling-Mark, Daily Chart from July 1, 1992, to November 12, 1992. This is an example of a market in a strong downward trend. (*Source:* Bloomberg L.P.)

trading partners tend to be more stable than those between minor trading partners. Trends that move slowly and steadily tend to be easier to trade than those that have more volatile intermediate moves.

The role of the central bank in controlling these trends will differ from country to country. This is illustrated by the contrasting approaches of the Bank of England and Germany's Bundesbank. Although the Bank of England is separate from the government, it will generally follow the ruling party's wishes. For instance, interest rates in the United Kingdom may be lowered leading up to election time. This has been evident in the past as interest rates have been eased to accommodate a Conservative party that is facing an upcoming election. On the other hand, the Bundesbank is not politicized. A good example can be seen in the recent high interest rates in Germany, even though the economy there is starting to slow, and politicians are calling for monetary ease. In this environment, the Bundesbank's response has been to keep rates high to control inflation. The bank's role is to keep inflation under control, at the expense of the economy and the politicians, and they have done a very good job of it.

THE ERM AND OTHER EXCHANGE RATE AGREEMENTS

Exchange rate agreements can come in all sorts of different forms, from a simple "gentlemen's agreement" between the central banks of two countries to a multilateral, fixed-rate exchange mechanism. Variations on the former have come and gone, and history has shown how easily they can be broken. The most successful example of the multilateral exchange system has been the semifixed exchange rate system of the European Monetary System, known as the Exchange Rate Mechanism (ERM).

Discussing exchange rate mechanisms is difficult, however, without at least paying homage to perhaps the most widely accepted exchange rate mechanism in history. While the world has now evolved away from the gold standard, in the minds of many it remains a viable standard to which we should return. The gold standard did not suddenly disappear in the early 1970s; several forces had been chipping away at it for some time, and the Nixon administration gave the final push. From the turn of the century to the Depression era, the United States adhered firmly to an exchange standard of $21 for one ounce of gold. Many industrialized countries emerged from World War I battered but still willing to carry the standard. Yet by 1933, most countries—except the United States and Switzerland—that were part of the standard had left it, depreciating or devaluing their units and replacing the stability of a gold link with quotas and a myriad of protectionist currency regulations. At that time, the Federal Reserve decided a similar devaluation was in order. It elected to stay with the gold standard, however, now requiring $35 to obtain one ounce of the yellow metal. But this came with some strings attached: the government also outlawed any tendering of goods or services with gold or transactions linked to gold.

In 1945, following the agreement coming out of the Bretton Woods Conference, the European countries and Canada rejoined the United States in the gold standard, but this time in a workable system. In this system, each country's currency held a "par value" against gold, a value from which it could only stray plus/minus 1%. This did not make for exciting times for a cross-rate trader. Currencies would be kept within this band through market intervention by its central bank. If the currency still appeared out of control, the country had to get permission from the governing international body, the International Monetary Fund (IMF) to repeg the value. Relying on the postwar surplus in exports, the U.S. government had begun to freely spend billions of U.S. dollars overseas. This chicken came home to roost, in that enormous amounts of U.S. dollars were now held in hands overseas, and what the Fed feared most was an international crisis that would cause a simultaneous demand for gold in U.S. reserves, which had greatly diminished. Throughout the 1960s, various measures were taken to limit the expenditure and export of U.S. dollars overseas. In late 1971, President Nixon both ordered the Fed to quit exchanging gold for dollars and to devalue the dollar against gold. This was the first step toward a full floating of the dollar. Within a year-and-a-half, most other countries followed suit and floated their currencies as well. In 1976, the dollar was deemed officially "floating" by an act of Congress.

Freedom from gold notwithstanding, many European nations had grown quite fond of currency stability. In the late 1970s, as the Bretton Woods club—led by gold and the U.S. dollar—was now well out of business, members of the European Community (EC) decided to form their own club, the European Monetary System. Two ideas dominated the EC resolution of 1979: (1) a method for controlling and fixing exchange rates between member countries—the Exchange Rate Mechanism (also known as the "grid" or the ERM); (2) the concept of a Continent-wide unit of exchange—the ECU. The grid would govern the limits of appreciation or depreciation of one member currency versus another. The resolution called for original and veteran members to hold to a 2.25% fluctuation, while new members enjoyed 6.0% for the first year or two of their participation. As for the Ecu, the drafters of the resolution did not take long to realize their hopes of a pan-Europe currency would not be realized soon. At this writing, the Ecu is still far from the pockets of the average European. On the other hand, it has enjoyed almost surprising popularity as a means of denomination for bond issues of various countries, especially those exhibiting higher interest rates or inflationary troubles. As shown in Figure 3–9, which breaks down the contributions of member currencies, the Ecu is essentially half D-mark and French franc.

European countries moving toward currency union have had a rocky history of cooperation. This move has been approached from two different viewpoints. The first is based on cooperation among sovereign states toward common goals, while the other assumes integration under

---

This effective limits analysis assumes that all currencies except the one under consideration will remain constant relative to each other.

Composition of the ECU (as of September 21, 1989):

Currency	*Amount of Currency*		*Currency Weight*
German Mark	DM	0.6242	30.3%
French Franc	FF	1.332	19.3%
British Pound	BP	0.08784	11.9%
Italian Lira	IL	151.80	10.2%
Dutch Guilder	NG	0.2198	9.5%
Belgian Franc	BF	3.301	7.8%
Spanish Peseta	SP	6.885	5.1%
Danish Krone	DK	0.1976	2.5%
Irish Pound	IP	0.008552	1.1%
Greek Drachma	GD	1.44	1.0%
Portuguese Escudo	PE	1.393	0.9%
Luxembourg Franc	LF	0.13	0.3%
			100.0%

Figure 3–9 The Composition of the ECU. (*Source:* Bloomberg L.P.)

a supranational federal power. The divisive issues evolving from this co-operation have pitted country against country within the Community. Complete monetary union in Europe is scheduled to arrive by 1999, but with the recent turmoil within the ERM, the prospects for a timely currency union in Europe seem remote.

In its final form, monetary union is essentially a fixing of exchange rates, which can be accomplished in one of two ways. First, a common currency can be used by different states, in a structure similar to that in the United States. The second option is to keep the individual currencies intact, but make them fully interchangeable at a irrevocably fixed rate. Whichever method is used, each state must give up individual control of its monetary and exchange rate policy. This is a political decision as much as it is an economic one.

The countries that participate in the EMS are all the current EC countries except Greece, Portugal, Britain, and Italy; they include Germany, France, Holland, Belgium, Denmark, Ireland, and Spain. Until September 1992, Britain and Italy had been participants, but they have suspended their involvement at this time. As of this writing, the system is in a state of flux, and its future direction is unclear. These currencies had been fixed in a band so their value would not fluctuate outside a predefined limit against other currencies in the grid. These limits were fluctuations of approximately 2.25% above and below a parity level for each of the currencies, except the British pound and Spanish peseta, where the limit was 6%. These bands may be adjusted, a topic that will be covered in a later chapter. When an EMS currency reaches its limit against another currency, the central banks of both countries will intervene to support the weak currency. This can be accomplished by direct purchases or sales in the foreign exchange markets, or by adjusting interest rates to encourage a change in capital flows. The most current exchange rate boundaries are described in Figure 3–10.

To the novice technical trader, these markets may seem to be perfect "trading range" markets because they have generalized upper and lower limits that are obeyed unless something extreme occurs. The technical discussion in Chapter 5 tackles this phenomenon. In short, exchange rate levels in the ERM can always fall prey to realignments, which can incur profitable opportunities or substantial losses depending on the position taken. In either case, for an ERM currency near its range limit with any other currency in the grid, an adjustment will occur either in the form of a realignment or an interest rate adjustment.

EMS CURRENCIES	LATEST SPOT RATE	CENTRAL PARITY & INTERVENTION LIMITS vs. DM		
		Upper Limit	Central Parity	Lower Limit
Belgian Franc	20.550	21.095	20.626	20.166
Danish Krone	3.8332	3.9016	3.8144	3.7300
Dutch Guilder	1.1238	1.1524	1.1267	1.1017
French Franc	3.3879	3.4305	3.3539	3.2792
Irish Punt	2.6109	2.6190	2.6789	2.7400
Italian Lira (suspended)	863.26			
Portuguese Escudo	89.130	92.340	86.940	81.900
Spanish Peseta	70.686	72.622	68.421	64.430
British Pound (susp.)	2.4425			

Figure 3–10 EMS Currencies with Central Parity Levels, Upper and Lower Intervention Boundaries, as of November 1, 1992.

PLAYING THE YIELDS

The discussion of interest rate differentials introduces another general class of cross rates: those that pit high-yield currencies against low-yield units. Generally, a high-yield currency is one that pays a higher rate of interest for holding it. It is important to remember that a purchase of a currency is the same as investing in that country's short-term money market. Therefore, a high-yield currency is one that has a high interest rate relative to some benchmark. For American traders, this would be any currency that pays a higher rate than the U.S. money market rate. European traders generally view the D-mark as the benchmark, so a high-yield currency in Europe is one with a higher interest rate than that of Germany. In the past, any currency carrying an interest rate higher than 8.5% has been considered a high yielder. As time goes by, and global interest rate levels change, this benchmark must also be adjusted up or down. The interest rate differential can be measured as the difference between two countries' short-term rates, charted over time. Figures 3–11 through 3–13 present interest rate differentials for three key cross rates.

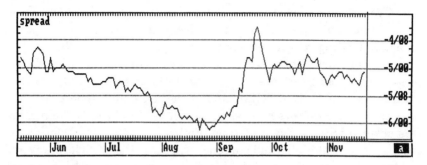

Figure 3–11   Three-Month Interest Rate Differential, Japan versus Germany, from May 1992 to November 1992. (*Source:* Telerate)

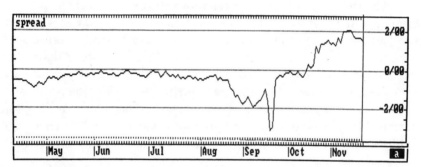

Figure 3–12   Three-Month Interest Rate Differential, Germany versus Britain, from May 1992 to November 1992. (*Source:* Telerate)

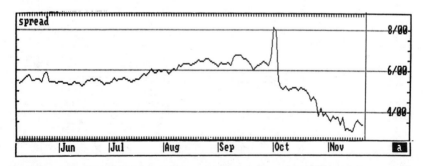

Figure 3–13   Three-Month Interest Rate Differential, Japan versus Britain, from May 1992 to November 1992. (*Source:* Telerate)

Traders must be cautious when buying a particular currency for the positive carry alone. Here the requirement before jumping in is not an active trading relationship between the two countries, but merely that one currency is paying a higher short-term interest rate. Examples of high-yield cross rates are crosses involving the Spanish peseta, Italian lira, Australian dollar, and Canadian dollar. These are now considered high yielders relative to the United States or Germany, but this pattern will change over time. Figures 3–14 to 3–17 show yield curves for several high-yield currencies against those of Germany and the United States. Some of the low-yield currencies at this time are the U.S. dollar, the Hong Kong dollar, and the Japanese yen. From a trading perspective, the strategy is fairly straightforward. The high-yield currency is purchased, while a low-yield currency is sold. The trader then captures the difference between the two rates.

The risk here is that the cross rate will move against the position by more than the interest that is earned. In fact, there may be a propensity for these rates to move more than a neutral carry trade. Figure 3–18 illustrates this in sterling-yen. Traders wishing to capture the higher interest rates in England relative to Japan would purchase pounds with yen. The figure shows this cross rate during 1992 when the pound suspended its ERM participation. Traders who had been long sterling-yen during this time would have suffered an extreme loss. The cross rate fell by much more than the approximate 6% interest rate differential.

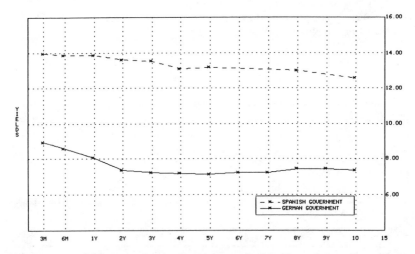

Figure 3–14 Yield Curve for Spain Compared with That of Germany. (*Source:* Bloomberg L.P.)

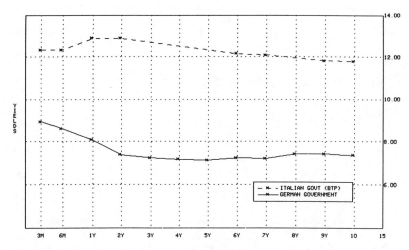

Figure 3–15 Yield Curve for Italy Compared with That of Germany. (*Source:* Bloomberg L.P.)

Because of this volatility, many traders view this type of trading as a short-term vehicle for holding money, but only during quiet trading times. For example, a trader may not believe that the market is going to move much over the next week and so will liquidate yen in favor of British pounds and hold them for that week.

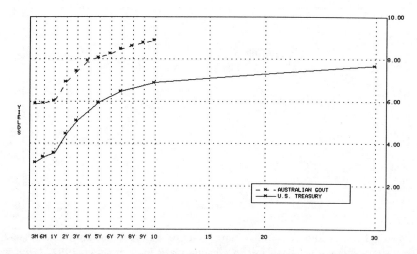

Figure 3–16 Yield Curve for Australia Compared with That of the United States. (*Source:* Bloomberg L.P.)

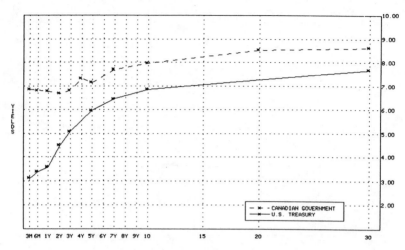

Figure 3–17 Yield Curve for Canada Compared with That of the United States. (*Source:* Bloomberg L.P.)

One can similarly play the long end of the yield curve. In "convergence trades" bond investors buy high-yielding bonds with low interest rate currency. Getting back to cross rates, the value of the high-yielding bonds can additionally be hedged by shorting the high-yielding currency. One who purchases Spanish bonds with borrowed D-marks, for instance, could sell pesetas against D-marks.

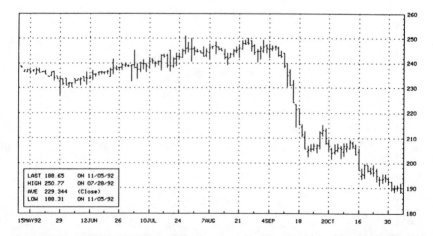

Figure 3–18 Sterling-Yen, Daily Chart from May 12, 1992, to November 5, 1992. This chart shows the sharp fall in sterling-mark in September 1992. (*Source:* Bloomberg L.P.)

4

FUNDAMENTALS OF FOREIGN EXCHANGE

INTRODUCTION

There exist as many methods of forecasting moves in currencies as there are forces moving these markets. Forecasting future moves can involve analyzing the forces themselves, or generalizing about patterns in price behavior. Before studying these markets, it is useful to consider what moves foreign exchange rates in general. The reader may ask, Why place a section of this size and scope in the middle of a book focused on trading cross rates, not on market fundamentals, which is a subject incidental to implementing the trade? However, the fundamental and economic factors behind exchange rate movements are even more important when discussing cross rates. There are several major factors, and many less important ones, but they all have something ridiculously obvious in common: The foreign exchange markets move when some force makes one currency either more or less valuable than another.

Demand for a currency can depend on the purchases of goods and services of that country or of assets denominated in that currency. Purchasers of goods are most often importers and exporters, such as a purchaser of parts from a Spanish steel components manufacturer for incorporation into a German engine. Purchasers of assets range from banks, money managers, and pension fund managers to corporate financial officers and wealthy individuals. A U.S. money manager, for instance, may have elected to purchase Dutch government bonds or Japanese stocks. The class of foreign exchange speculators probably includes yourself, as well as banks, money managers, wealthy individuals, and trading advisors.

The cumulative purchases and sales of a currency cause it to move up or down and to become more or less valuable than another currency. The reasons behind the purchases and sales can be broadly classified into two categories: economic factors and confidence factors. Under the economic category, some analysts believe a distinction exists between economic indicators explaining a past event and indicators used to try and predict a future one. Whichever camp you are in, your goal is to explain real-life phenomena. Economic approaches examine the demand stemming from purchases of goods, services, or assets. Confidence factors, on the other hand, are general and often nonquantitative explanations for a past or prospective market move, and can include market sentiment about the management of a country's currency or hunches concerning other players in the market. These approaches examine speculative demand rather than economic demand.

A factor contributing to the pricing of cross rates is interest rate differentials between the two countries. Consequently, we should examine the concept of cost of carry. On a very basic level, an investment in a foreign currency is essentially an investment in the money market of that country. For example, a U.S.-based trader who buys German marks is actually investing in the German money market and thus will earn interest on the money at German rates. If rates in Germany are higher than those in the U.S., the trader would benefit by holding D-marks relative to U.S. dollars. This is called *positive carry* since the interest rate differential between the currencies is positive. For example, assume that interest rate in Germany is 8.5%, and the interest rate in the United States is 4%. This is a difference of 4.5%, and the buyer of marks earns this differential over time by holding marks. The trader is effectively borrowing at 4%, by shorting the dollar, and lending at 8.5%, by buying the mark. On the other hand, if U.S. interest rates were higher than German rates, the same transaction would involve *negative carry,* and it would cost the trader 4.5% per year to hold dollars against the mark. These differentials are very important in determining which currency to hold. All else being equal, an investor typically will buy the currency with the higher yield, and sell the one with the lower yield, to earn the carry.

While the strict market technician could probably skim over this chapter on fundamentals, recent history shows how ignoring a country's economics altogether may not be a good idea. In late 1991, for example, in the D-mark/Finnish markka cross, the mark-Finn rate was very strong; that is, the mark was strong and the Finn was weak. The Finnish government was forced to defend its currency by keeping interest rates high, hovering around 15%. Many traders decided to hold Finnish markka in order to realize the higher yield on the currency. Their view was that the Finnish government would hold the line on currency devaluation as it always had in the past. This approach held up for some time, and traders were rewarded handsomely. However, as unemployment remained high and a recession began to appear in Finland, the government was forced to act. They devalued the Finn to bring it back into line. Interest rates, which had spiked to near 20%, fell immediately to below 10%. Any traders caught on the wrong side took heavy losses. This movement can be seen in Figure 4–1. The traders' reasons for staying in may have been technical or quantitative, but they also were accompanied by a disregard for economics. The lesson to be learned here is that even strict market technicians must remember some fundamental considerations.

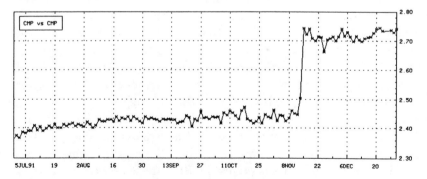

Figure 4–1   Mark-Finn Markka, Daily Cross-Rate Chart from July 1, 1991, to December 31, 1991. This shows the devaluation of the markka, or revaluation of the mark. This was an overnight move that took the mark-Finn from 2.45 DM/FM to 2.74 DM/FM. It was impossible to execute a trade during the move, which effectively took place in a matter of minutes. (*Source:* Bloomberg L.P.)

As always, there's no such thing as a free lunch. To earn the higher Finnish rates, traders were taking the high risk of devaluation. Most traders thought they were getting a great deal and earning unusually high interest rates, but they were left holding a devalued currency. They counted on past behavior of the Finnish government in assuming it would adhere to the current exchange-rate levels. An astute trader may have realized that high rates for low risk was too good to be true. As explained later in this chapter, the moral of the story is—because the markets are fairly efficient at pricing risk—traders must take risks to play carry markets.

ECONOMIC FACTORS

Economic factors usually affect a currency by altering the interest rate structure of the country. Many economists would be more general, saying a currency depends on the purchases of goods, services, and assets denominated in that currency. Nonetheless, while a connection does exists between demand for goods and demand for currency, most market analysts agree a stronger connection exists with demand for assets. In Chapter 2, we briefly explained the link between exchange rates and interest rates. The interest rate structure of a country, however, could reflect perhaps an even more important structure—the overall monetary health of that country.

Other economic, specifically macroeconomic, factors also come into play—often overriding carry considerations—in the next aspect of examining interest rate differentials: the *expected direction* of interest rates. Traders of any market know that expected changes in conditions hold as much weight, if not more, than the actual changes. Here, any change in the economic outlook that will result in higher rates will also result in the higher value of that country's currency, vis-à-vis the rest of the world. For example, if unemployment is dropping sharply in Germany as it begins an economic expansion, but remains fairly high in Britain, where the economy is lagging, the demand for money in Germany can be expected to go up. All of this will result in higher interest rates in Germany relative to those in Britain; if everything else remains constant, the mark should rise against the pound as the mark becomes relatively more valuable. An attentive trader could profit by buying the mark and selling the pound.

These expectations can, to a certain extent, be measured by yield curves. A yield curve is simply the relationship between short-term interest rates and long-term interest rates, expressed graphically. Each maturity is plotted on a chart and a picture of interest rate expectations is generated. Figure 4–2 shows the yield curve in the United States in late 1992. Since each country has different interest rates and expectations, their yield curves will be somewhat different. Compare the yield curves of Japan and Sweden with that of the United States (see Figures 4–3 and 4–4). There are three distinct pictures of interest rate expectations. In the first, interest rates are expected to increase over time. In the second, rates are expected to remain fairly constant for about three years, and then trend upward. In contrast, in the last one, they are expected to fall. A yield curve where interest rates increase with time is called a normal curve. One where interest rates are expected to fall is called an inverted curve. Normally, there is some risk premium associated with holding longer term investments, so a normal curve is upward sloping. However, if expectations are for falling rates, this may offset the duration risk premium, and the curve may invert.

The next question is, What does this tell us about the direction of currency prices? Unfortunately, the answer is not definitive. On a short-term basis, the shape of the yield curve will not accurately forecast the direction of currency movements. What can be helpful, however, is to view yield curves as they change. For example, when England suspended its participation in the Exchange Rate Mechanism (ERM) in September 1992, its curve shifted from inverted to normal, as the Bank

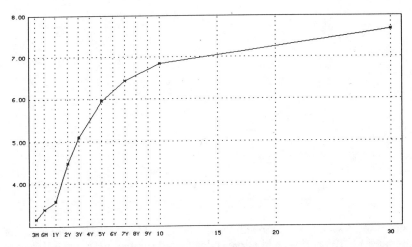

Figure 4–2　U.S. Treasury Yield Curve, 3 Months to 30 Years, as of November 12, 1992. (*Source:* Bloomberg L.P.)

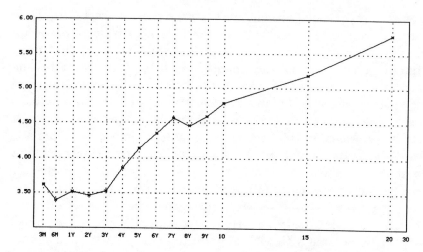

Figure 4–3 Japanese Government Yield Curve, 3 Months to 30 Years, as of November 12, 1992. The yield curve is flat through 3 years, and then upward sloping. (*Source:* Bloomberg L.P.)

of England was no longer pressured to keep short-term interest rates high to defend the pound. This shift in expectations also hit the currency markets, as the sterling-mark lost value simultaneously.

Many different economic factors that can affect interest rates, and these factors are of particular concern to foreign-exchange traders

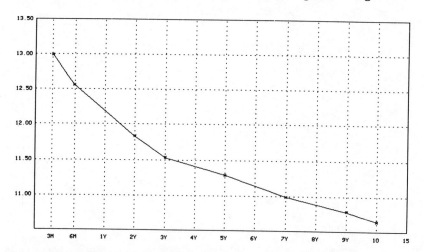

Figure 4–4 Swedish Government Yield Curve, 3 Months to 10 Years, as of November 12, 1992. This yield curve is downward sloping, or inverted. (*Source:* Bloomberg L.P.)

trying to forecast the direction of exchange rates. One of the more prominent factors influencing interest rates is the rate of inflation. Investors will hold a currency to earn interest only if the currency has high real interest returns, not just high nominal interest rates. For example, if interest rates in France are 1% higher than those in Belgium, but the inflation rate is 2% higher in France, then real interest rates are actually higher in Belgium. Thus, the inflation figures of a country can serve as indicators of the direction of exchange rates. In general, inflation is associated with a falling currency. Higher rates of inflation, however, can make the currency go either up or down. While this seems strange at first glance, it rings true in many situations. An analyst can look at two important aspects of a currency's reaction to economic conditions: short term versus long term, and expectations theory.

Comparison of the short term and the long term examines the impact of economic stimulus over differing time horizons. The preceding inflation example is a case in point. In the long run, a higher inflation rate is usually bad for the economy and therefore a negative for the currency. However, in the short run, if France's inflation rate were to increase, and the French government answered by raising its interest rates to maintain the real interest yield, the market may force the French franc higher. Thus, as a positive carry trade, the franc would become more valuable. On the other hand, in time the franc may fall if the Bank of France does not raise interest rates.

The theory that interest rate differentials between two currencies determine the exchange rate is currently back in vogue. At other times, many analysts and traders have been fixated to a similar degree on other things such as money supply numbers, trade balances or unemployment reports. As an example, in the mid-1980s, the weekly releases of money supply numbers would cause a sharp reaction in the credit and currency markets. Later, the release of Merchandise Trade Balance numbers caused the markets to react violently as traders waited to see how bad the deficit was. A large number of them now are watching worldwide interest rate markets to determine their positioning in the currency markets. True, the fundamental connection between interest rates and exchange rates appears more casual, but analysts must still be cautious. Over the long term, interest rate changes account for only a small percentage of the overall movements of currency prices. Research conducted by GK Capital, for instance, attempted to test this causal relationship. Using different lag times, the study concluded that changes in interest rate differentials between the U.S. dollar and the D-mark corresponded to only 17% of the movement in the dollar-mark exchange rate, while the dollar-yen differential accounted for only 8% of its currency movement. As for the impact of the release of important economic data, including those reports and releases mentioned earlier, further research revealed only an effect so small it could be deemed statistically insignificant. So, in the short term, the price might move sharply, but in the longer term, the numbers seem to have no noticeable impact. Interestingly, what did seem to matter was the market's expectation of what the economic release would be. For instance, a release that would normally have been interpreted as being bullish for the dollar, may have actually hurt it if traders were expecting an even better number.

These results demand that any discussion of inflation and interest rates include another factor, expectations of market participants. Using the earlier example, if market participants expect a higher rate of inflation or see signs of higher rates of inflation, then they may also anticipate the bank of France raising interest rates. If rates are not raised, the French franc will likely depreciate. Thus expectations alone may cause movements in the exchange rates.

Consequently, market players are always watching for indications of monetary policy, or more importantly, changes in monetary policy. Another important sign for monetary policy is money supply. Money supply can be measured in several ways. One country's measure of money supply will measure different things than another's. In the United States, these measures are given the definitions M1, M2, and M3. The M1 definition is the most narrow and includes all assets that the public normally uses directly for transactions, including paper and coin money, money in checking accounts, other demand deposits, and traveler's checks. M2 is a broader measure that includes M1 as well as overnight repurchase agreements, certain overnight Eurodollar deposits, money market mutual funds, savings accounts not included in M1, and money market deposit accounts. M3 is the broadest measure. It includes M2 plus certain other funds. The Federal Reserve uses these different measures to monitor the amount of money in circulation, and the money supply figures are closely watched by traders. In fact, M1 was watched so closely in the early 1980s that the market would react violently to the release of the data. It then moved into the background as traders focused on other indicators, most notably the balance of trade and, more recently, the unemployment data. However, as of this writing, many traders are once again focusing on money supply, specifically M2, as a clue to future Fed moves.

Generally, interest rates are a function of money supply, because, in the most simple definition, the interest rate is a measure of the demand for money. Going back to a basic supply-demand analysis, as demand for money increases, interest rates will rise. Several factors can cause this shift in demand, many of which are related to the strength of the economy. As an economy strengthens, the demand for money increases and the interest rates should move higher. Following along with this analysis, the currency of that country should also move higher.

The central bank of a country will manipulate the money supply in that country in different ways. In the United States, supply of money is what M1 and M2 measure, and that is what the U.S. Federal Reserve can directly control. If the supply curve shifts outward, interest rates will fall. The Fed usually controls the money supply by injecting reserves into the economy or withdrawing them through purchases or sales of securities. If the Fed purchases these, it is paying for them with funds that are not initially included in the money supply, thereby adding funds to the system and increasing money supply.

Another tool the Fed uses to control interest rates is much more direct: a change in the U.S. discount rate. This is the rate that banks must pay to borrow money from the Fed overnight. A move in this rate will directly affect the level of interest rates. This move is rather bold and used less frequently than the daily reserve compensations. As for foreign central banks, they generally use this technique to control their interest rates and currencies as well. In the past, foreign central banks have usually adjusted their base rates between two and five times per year. These moves are very closely watched by traders in cross rates.

One source of demand for currency that was mentioned earlier is the demand for goods and services. As the focus for reports related to trade, the goods market was the origin of most of those disruptive U.S. government releases in the late 1980s, especially the U.S. trade balance numbers. Trade data can also yield a cache of information for long-term forecasts of currencies, at least for those who can make some genuine sense of it. Most economists have had more success employing trade-related economic data as the input for long-term barometers of the intrinsic value of a currency. Trade flows are reflected in measures of not only the trade balance but a country's current account deficit as well.

One of the most popular long-term indicators of late incorporates trade flows. The purchasing price parity (PPP) measure is actually a *very* long-term indicator. A PPP level tries to estimate an appropriate value for exchange rate between currencies X and Y by working backward from discrepancies in actual prices of comparable goods in the two countries. Put another way, the theory says that in the long run, goods and services should cost the same in real terms. For example, if the price of a new car is worth 6 months' wages in one country, it should be worth 6 months' wages in every country. If this is not the case, and it is usually not, then there is a discrepancy in purchasing power parity. While not a terribly precise measurement, nearly everyone in the international markets has become acquainted with the "Big Mac Index" compiled and published monthly in the *Economist,* where the editors list the exchange rates between the United States and various countries based on local prices of this relatively consistent fast food product.

While the PPP offers an interesting measure of the long-term "value" of a currency, it has largely fallen out of favor with economists. Nonetheless, as Figures 4–5 through 4–7 illustrate, it may be something traders want to keep at least on the back burner. At first glance, plots of an exchange rate often appear to regress toward the exchange rate's PPP measure, particularly in markets like the mark-Swiss rate, which seems habitually to regress toward the PPP mean. But in many

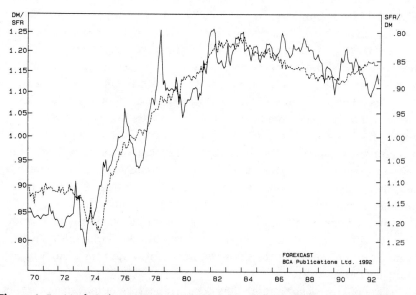

Figure 4–5 Mark-Swiss, 1970 to 1992. The cross rate (solid line) seems to regress toward the PPP mean (dashed line). (*Source:* FOREXCAST, BCA Publications Ltd.)

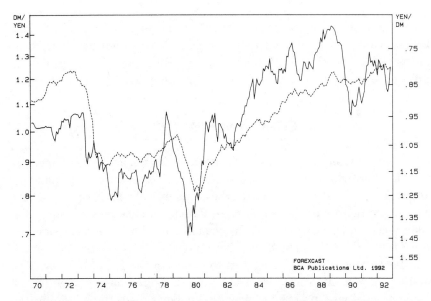

Figure 4–6   Mark-Yen, 1970 to 1992. The cross rate (solid line) seems to regress toward the PPP mean (dashed line). However, there are times, such as the mid-1980s, where there are long-lasting separations. (*Source:* FOREXCAST, BCA Publications Ltd.)

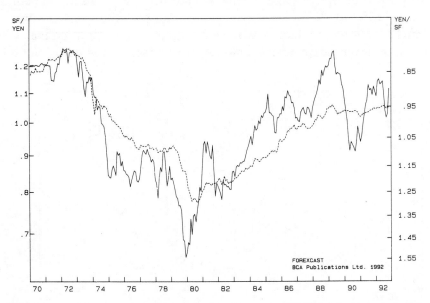

Figure 4–7   Swiss-Yen, 1970 to 1992. The cross rate (solid line) is compared with the PPP mean (dashed line). (*Source:* FOREXCAST, BCA Publications Ltd.)

other markets, a divergence from the PPP's measure of "value" can last for years and even several entire business cycles. As an illustration, look at the years 1983 through 1989 in Figure 4–6 (mark-yen). A significant difference in the cross rate and the PPP mean existed for several years.

CONFIDENCE FACTORS

Confidence factors, in contrast to economic factors, are largely qualitative. Earlier, when we discussed the power of expectations in the market, those expectations dealt with the economics of a market. Almost all confidence factors are expectations-related. An excellent example of a confidence factor at work could be seen during the British elections in April 1992. Over the months leading up to the elections, the Conservative Party steadily lost its lead in the polls to the Labour Party. The market viewed this very negatively, since Labour was not regarded as being probusiness. Its tax and spending policies made the UK financial markets very jittery. As Labour gained in the polls, the sterling-mark cross was holding near its lower band within the ERM. The expectation was that there would be dramatic pound weakness on a Labour victory. Just one week before the elections, Labour had a 7% lead in the polls and sterling-mark was under pressure. The best the Conservatives could hope for was a hung parliament with a Labour coalition majority. In a dramatic comeback, however, the Conservatives pulled out a

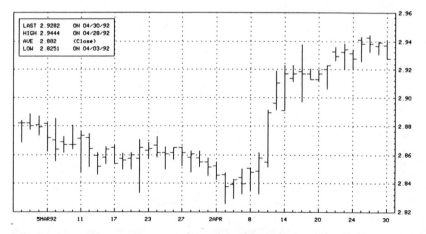

Figure 4–8 Sterling-Mark, Daily Chart from March 2, 1992, to April 30, 1992. This shows the reaction in the foreign exchange markets to a surprise election victory by the British Conservative party. (*Source:* Bloomberg L.P.)

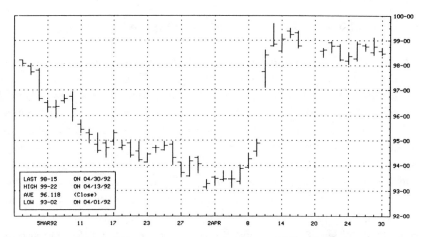

Figure 4-9 British Gilts, June Futures Contract, Daily Chart from March 2, 1992, to April 30, 1992. This shows the reaction in the bond markets to a surprise election victory by the British Conservative party. (*Source:* Bloomberg L.P.)

narrow majority. Since expectations had been leaning toward a lower cross rate, many players were short sterling-mark. As the surprise victory unfolded, sterling rallied sharply. Figures 4–8 through 4–10 show the reaction to the Conservative victory in the currency, bond, and stock markets of England. This example clearly illustrates the way a market reacts to news.

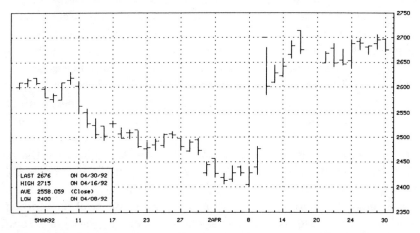

Figure 4-10 Financial Times Stock Index (FTSI 100), June Futures Contract, Daily Chart from March 2, 1992, to April 30, 1992. This shows the reaction in the equity markets to a surprise election victory by the British Conservative party. (*Source:* Bloomberg L.P.)

BUILDING A WORKABLE CROSS-RATES MODEL

Constructing an econometric model for trading currencies does not necessarily require a degree in economics. What it does demand is some understanding of certain terms along with a great deal of faith in economists and their science. This statement alone might cause readers to skip ahead to the next section, but we will try to keep this discussion relevant. The information already presented in this chapter, for the most part, forms the basis for the standard fare provided by the traditional econometric forecasters and their assortment of related publications. The following methodologies serve as examples of the kind of things you should expect from such services. Good news, however, for the staunch do-it-yourselfers: We are not economists. Each of the following methodologies can be calculated and tracked using two tools: Lotus 1-2-3 or similar spreadsheet programs, and a reliable source for economic data on various countries. In fact, some of you may want only to skim this section. It is an exercise in constructing some long-term econometric forecasts but is not overly useful for trading because, in practice, it is difficult to trade on a very long-term basis. That being said, it is still important to understand the basic building blocks for analysis of currency valuations.

Survey the market of econometric services and you'll find that most of their modeling constitutes variations on the relationships explained earlier, incorporating both economic and confidence factors. Most econometric models appear to emphasize the link between interest rates and inflation. Many of these, however, consist of a "black box"-type of approach that their creators find difficult to explain without using terribly esoteric language and a great deal of math. Nonetheless, some of the best market economists have been able not only to construct an intelligent model but to convey at least the basics of its underpinnings. One group that can do this is the editors of the *Bank Credit Analyst* (BCA), and we will review their analysis technique. The Montreal-based group's currency model comprises 75% fundamental indicators, the remainder incorporating technically oriented momentum indicators. According to the group, the fundamentals portion must always consist of the output of two main components, a long-term measure of *value* in conjunction with a medium-term measure of *monetary growth* of a country's economy. The long-term value component can comprise one item, such as trade flows or the PPP mentioned earlier, or a combination of valuation theories. For long-term value, the group has chosen to look at the fiscal health of the two countries underlying a foreign exchange rate by tracking the "net indebtedness" of the countries. The monetary and growth component concentrates on the credit liquidity of a country and its effect on economic growth. In perhaps oversimplified terms, movements in the exchange rate between two countries can be forecasted in the medium term by looking at availability of credit, while the long-term value is determined by the amount of debt (see Figure 4–11).

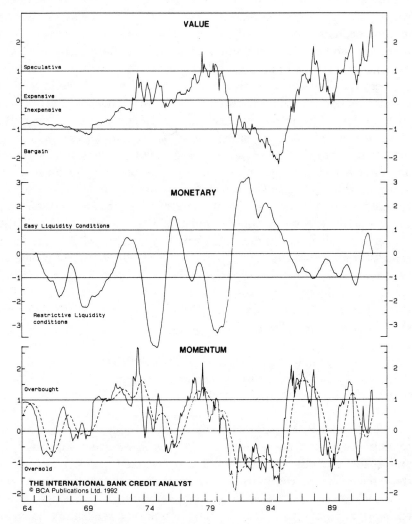

Figure 4–11   D-Mark Currency Model Components, Showing the Value Component, the Monetary Component and the Momentum Component. (*Source:* FOREXCAST, BCA Publications Ltd.)

LONG-TERM ECONOMIC INDICATORS

Using the preceding approach toward fundamentals—long-term value and medium-term monetary analyses—we must pick apart or at least illustrate the indicators and methodologies that operate as either type of analysis. In trying to determine the long-term value of one currency in terms of another, the BCA group is not alone in believing that the countries' respective fiscal conditions may act as gauges. The indebtedness of a particular economy affects the long-term attractiveness of that economy's assets—especially its stock and long-term bond markets—and the country's industrial capacity. Both attractive asset markets and strong industry need to be present in order to attract foreign capital. Inflows of foreign capital mean higher demand for that country's current. When a group of armchair economists argue over what serves as the actual, bottom line "value"of a currency, the PPP is often mentioned. The PPP level between two countries is probably the most tempting measure because it is so easy to understand. As previously explained, the measure rests on the notion of parity of consumer and wholesale prices in two countries. What else could make such intuitive sense? But the overall debt outstanding (relative to the rest of the world) of the two countries must play some role. BCA's "Value Component" shown in Figure 4–11 actually consists of two indicators, the PPP and something the group calls a "Debt Proxy" between the two countries, which incorporates the respective current account deficits as compared with the respective domestic production (see Figure 4–12). The BCA calculates the Debt Proxy as follows ("G" denotes the German figures, "US," the American):

$$DP_{\text{G-US}} = (CCA^{\text{G}}/GDP_{\text{G}}) - (CCA^{\text{US}}/GDP_{\text{US}})$$
$$CCA = \text{cumulative current account}$$
$$GDP = \text{gross domestic product}$$

The Debt Proxies for both dollar-mark and dollar-yen can be compared with the more traditional PPP determination. Figures 4–13 and 4–14 plot both against their respective currencies. The value of these models is not really from a trading perspective, but from an understanding perspective. If you can understand the concepts behind the analysis, you are well on the road to having a reasonable basis for fundamental analysis of the currency markets. Who knows, you may even be able to construct your own econometric models.

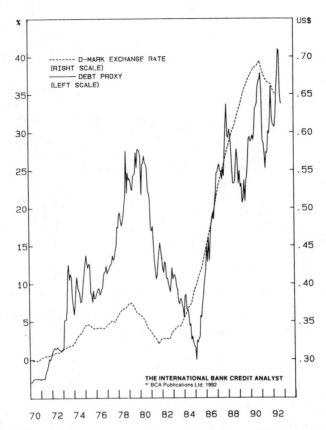

Figure 4–12 The Dollar-Mark Exchange Rate Compared with the Debt Proxy. The debt proxy is calculated as the German cumulated current account to GNP ratio, less the U.S. cumulated current account in GNP ratio. (*Source:* FOREXCAST, BCA Publications Ltd.)

MEDIUM-TERM ECONOMIC INDICATORS

Measurements of monetary growth also incorporate aspects of a country's capacity for freedom of capital. These normally form a more medium-term fundamental indicator. National economies walk a tightrope. An adequate degree of monetary liquidity is required for the expansion of any economy. Without liquidity, there is no investment; and without investment, there is no growth. On the other hand, as soon as growth occurs, the supply of money in an economy must not outpace growth. When it does, the inflation that results not only

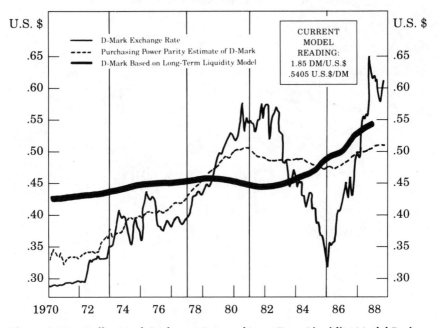

Figure 4–13 Dollar-Mark Exchange Rate and Long-Term Liquidity Model Projections. (*Source:* FOREXCAST, BCA Publications Ltd.)

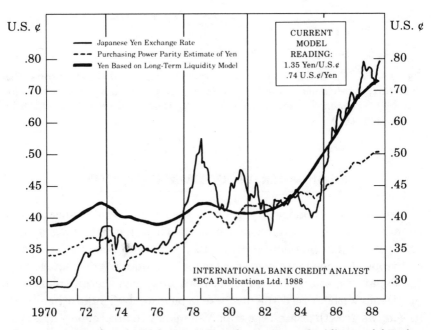

Figure 4–14 Dollar-Yen Exchange Rate and Long-Term Liquidity Model Projections. (*Source:* FOREXCAST, BCA Publications Ltd.)

removes liquidity by depleting savings but also contributes to the more long-term bearish factor touched on earlier, debt. As monetary authorities tighten an economy's purse strings, deflation usually ensues.

Medium-term fundamentals consist most often of various methods for determining on which side of the tightrope an economy is tipping, or at least if the inflation-deflation cycle is inevitable, in what part of the cycle a particular country's economy finds itself. One symptom traders could look at is inflation, some measure of change in wholesale or consumer prices. Like the contrast in national indebtedness of two economies made earlier, keep in mind that everything in exchange rate markets is relative. Therefore, why not simply create an index that analyzes the two countries' rates of inflation, perhaps analyzing the difference or the ratio between the two? Well, first of all, any present estimate of inflation, be it some consumer price index (CPI) or producer price index (PPI), actually measures the past. Accordingly, many economists would argue that the inflation rates are already taken into account in both the country's short-term interest rate markets and, consequentially, its currency.

An indicator that offers some forecast of inflation expected in the future, however, may be helpful. Accepting the age-old monetarist theory on inflation, future inflation in a country could be projected by analyzing the current rate or monetary growth versus that of some measure of overall economic growth. The idea is that, all other things equal, when monetary growth outstrips overall production a country gets an increase in the inflation rate. Production rates faster than that of monetary growth would result in a decrease in a country's inflation rate. The following indicator, expected change in inflation (ECI), is but one very simple way to gauge this relationship. It is far from comprehensive, however, as it does not incorporate important factors such as the money velocity in a country. The ECI employs a country's industrial production estimate as a barometer of the overall growth, and M1 as the measure of broad money supply.

$$EI = I + ECI$$

where

EI = Expected Inflation
I = the current 3-month interest rate, and
$ECI = \mathrm{Ln}((100 + M)/(100 + Prod))*K$

where

> Ln = the natural log (this turns quotients less than 1 into
> negative numbers, and those greater than 1 into
> positive numbers)
> M = annualized % decrease or growth in M1 for country
> x over one month
> $Prod$ = annualized % decrease or growth in industrial
> production of country x over one month, and
> K = the constant for country x.

Using Germany as an example, we examined the relationship be-tween monetary growth (M) and production (Prod) over time, and com-pared that to what occurred in German inflation rates nine months later. On February 1, 1991, for instance, growth in German M1 was 5.9%, while growth in production was 5.0%. Plugging these into the for-mula above would yield 0.85, as the quotient, times the constant K. The value 0.85 alone—as a positive number—serves as an indication that inflation should rise in the coming months.

The purpose of K is basically that of a coefficient connecting the money-production relationship with Germany's actual inflation months later. One can basically solve for K based on the historical information—the stuff of regression analysis. Because this is not meant to be a primer on statistics, however, we will refrain from expounding on regression analyses. A value of 0.52 for K appear to function as the coefficient fit-ting M and Prod to later inflation data. Using K, the formula would yield 0.85 times 0.52, or 0.45. This means that 0.45% can be added to the an-nualized inflation rate on February 1 (2.7%) to get an inflation rate ex-pected nine months later, November 1, of 3.15%. Trying to get a K that best fits the formula to actual data can sometimes yield imperfect re-sults. In real life, the German economy registered an inflation rate of 4.0% on November 1. Nonetheless, the ECI at least told us that inflation would be getting worse—and the currency weakening.

In applying all of this to the cross-rate context, a trader could use a ratio of two countries' estimates in an attempt to discern which of the two currencies may remain more stable. This could be accomplished by taking the ratio of expected inflation rates in the two countries. A for-mula to do this might be:

$$EI \text{ ratio}_{x-y} = EI_x / EI_y$$

To illustrate, let us take the expected inflations of two countries, Switzerland and Germany. The actual ratio (Germany/Swiss) on February 1, 1991, was 0.43 (2.7/6.3) while, in contrast, the ratio of EIs for nine months later was 0.64 (3.15/4.95). It would seem the formulas would have indicated that over the next few months, the Swiss franc was a much better unit than the D-mark. However, as illustrated by Figure 4–15, the mark was actually the better currency to own. One possible explanation for this goes back to expectations theory. The level of inflation in Germany was expected to remain high, and the German central bank was expected to keep interest rates high in order to control inflation. Because of these relatively high interest rates, the mark increased in value relative to the franc.

After this lengthy discussion on inflation, we return to a subject discussed earlier, interest rate differentials. Rather than using several complex formulas, why not simply compare differences in the short-term interest rates of the two countries? After all, people want to own those currencies providing a higher yield.

To reiterate, many economists believe an interest rate differential is a redundant and oversimplified restatement of the obvious, and perhaps even a product of movements in a particular exchange rate and not its cause. Economist Milton Friedman once commented that relatively higher short-term interest rates may actually be a strong sign of a *weak,*

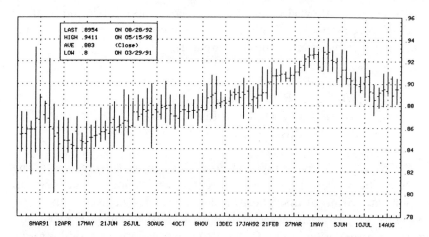

Figure 4–15 Mark-Swiss, Daily Chart from February 8, 1991, to August 28, 1992. The mark showed a slight increase relative to the franc over this time period. (*Source:* Bloomberg L.P.)

not attractive, currency. (After all, higher interest rates in a country usually indicates a problem of some sort, be it inflation or attraction of capital.) To obtain an improved measure, therefore, some analysts have given a new twist to differentials by employing *real* interest rate differentials. In other words, they plot the differences between short-term interest rates as discounted by the respective countries' present rates of inflation. The following calculation of real interest rates forms one elementary example:

$$RIR = IR - CPI$$
$$IR = \text{Nominal interest rate}$$
$$CPI = \% \text{ change (annualized) in the consumer price index}$$
$$\text{of that country (calculated monthly).}$$

But again, economists believe that since short-term interest-rates already take inflation into account, the analyst could be accused of pouring spice to an already spicy dish. The preceding formula also carries another weakness: It assumes the present rate of inflation will continue in the future. Many analysts are willing to make this assumption and allow the use of present estimates of inflation.

Others have gone a step farther, incorporating some estimate of expected inflation. That is, What if you subtracted *expected*, not *actual*, inflation from the current interest rate? These are called real interest rates. Our own estimate of Expected Change in Inflation (ECI) described earlier, allowed us to adjust present rates of inflation to arrive at the future estimate, EI. With this, one might plot out a time series of the following for several pairs of countries:

$$ERIR_x = IR_x - EI_x$$
$$ERIR \ diff_{x\text{-}y} = ERIR_x - ERIR_y$$
$$ERIR = \text{expected real interest rate}$$
$$ERIR \ diff = \text{difference between two countries' ERIRs}$$

Overall, the more sophisticated and successful cross-rate analysts in the market have ceased to rely on variations of short-term interest rate differentials. These traders are still focused on the money markets and returns associated with two different currencies, but with an alternative angle. One well-known example would be an approach comparing the entire spectrum of money and credit markets of two countries. Rather than merely contrasting short-term interest rates, this approach expands the comparison to differences in the two countries' yield curves, which we viewed earlier. As for fiddling around with the effects of inflation on these yields, economists agree that because inflation outlooks are already taken into account on the long end of the yield curve, there's not much point to coming up with your own. Comparing two different yield curves could consist of repeatedly applying some of the same analyses described earlier to the 30-, 10-, and 5-year bond yields in addition to the 3-month Eurorate. A simpler approach could consist of simply subtracting the short end from the long end, getting positive numbers for normally sloped yield curves and negative numbers for inverted yield curves.

$$YC = LBY - IR$$
$$YC\ diff = YC_x - YC_y$$
$$YC = \text{yield curve,}$$
$$LBY = \text{long-bond (30 years) yield.}$$
$$IR = \text{short-term interest rate}$$

But perhaps the most revealing source of information about the "yield" of a particular currency may be the interbank market itself. Many traders believe the forward rate associated with a currency tell more about what kind of yield a holder of that currency should expect than its short-term Eurorate, even extremely short-term Eurorates. You may recall the math behind calculation of premiums for bank forward contracts in Chapter 2. To review briefly, the principle of interest rate parity says that the premium (or discount) forward rate of exchange between currencies X and Y should approximate the difference between the short-term interest rates of X and Y of the same period. Say the 3-month Euromark is roughly 890 percentage points while the Euroyen rate offers 740; the interest rate differential is 250 points in favor of Germany. If mark-yen is going for 77.200, 250 points should correspond to a premium (if you're Japanese and buying D-marks) of 0.483. Looking at the forward market, the 3-month mark-yen forward trades at a premium of, sure enough, 0.483, or, in interbank parlance, a "standard" swap (forward minus spot) of 483. If it were much less, Japanese investors would become very excited and purchase spot D-marks in great quantities, deposit them in a German bank, and sell D-marks three months forward. They would essentially earn the full 250 points plus an extra few points. This, in turn, would bring the interest rate and forward markets back in line.

But why all this work if the standard swap leaves you with the same thing as the regular interest rate differential? What we have just looked at is the standard swap, one reflecting the interest rate for a chunk of time from the present to three months out. Now let us move forward in time. Next look at a "forward-forward" swap; for example, the 6-month forward minus a 3-month forward. This chunk of time hands us an implied 3-month Eurorate differential of 0.435, different from the earlier result. Traders with any experience trading intramarket spreads should be familiar with this process. What the market is saying is that three months from now the short-term interest rates between the two countries will narrow (from .483 to .435). Similarly, we could obtain a 9-month rate by analyzing the 3-month forward-12-month forward swap. We could continue and construct a large part of the yield curves for two countries for different points in the future.

Keep in mind that, amidst all the talk of arbitrage and interest rate returns, the whole point is to obtain something that improves your forecasting of moves in the currency, not to find arbitrage opportunities or to earn interest income. The preceding analyses serve as examples of another component for a workable model: the monetary and credit factors. It would be inappropriate to describe these analyses as "models" when they simply transform data into new forms of data. Several hundred different models could exist performing several hundred different operations on these data.

SOURCES FOR FUNDAMENTAL DATA

The trader intent on monitoring some of the relationships outlined in this chapter can obtain the necessary figures and other data from a number of sources. The interest rate markets, including the daily "fixes" of key rates, are included in almost any market data service, such as Telerate's and Reuters'. These data vendors usually include several electronic "pages" detailing the latest economic releases. Even services lacking such extensive economic coverage will, at a minimum, disseminate economic statistics as part of their news bulletins. The serious researcher or builder of econometric models, however, more than likely requires historical, as well as current, data. While some subscribers to news-oriented services have built their own database piecemeal by transcribing off the vendor's screen or downloading, this can be time-consuming. In North America, it is not hard to find vendors that provide economic indicators of the U.S. and Canadian economies, or other assorted fundamental data necessary for a U.S. or Canadian dollar-based foreign exchange model. Models built for the cross-currencies markets, however, demand a more multinational and comprehensive array of data. Unfortunately, data services that compile economic and money market data for Japan and the European countries are less common. One surprisingly thorough source is the back page of any issue of the *Economist*. Most of the preceding examples of long- and medium-term fundamental methodologies can be calculated using the figures listed every month in this British-based publication, and those patient enough can certainly compile a reliable database by digging through piles of back issues. Services that do provide useful data include Datastream International and, to a more limited extent, Dow Jones Irwin, International. Bodies such as the Organization for Economic and Cooperative Development (OECD) and the World Bank, both of which have offices in New York, provide most of the previously mentioned data on tape. Those engaging in large-scale, in-depth analysis often go straight to the source, the central banks themselves. The German Bundesbank and the Bank of England, for example, usually provide such figures on either an electronic or print medium at reasonable rates.

Datastream offers one of the more comprehensive examples of a service amenable to econometric modeling. Like some other services, Datastream provides economic news releases and is able to graphically depict time series of various markets or economic figures. However, the firm prides itself on its bank of price and economic data. These include actual data and percentage changes in short- and long-term interest rates of more than 18 countries, the inflation and industrial production for eight countries, and historical spot and forward on even minor cross-currency rates. In addition, the service offers a feature allowing subscribers to store and build on their own time series database.

5

TECHNICAL AND INTERMARKET ANALYSIS OF CROSS RATES

The title of the preceding chapter did not mention "cross rates" specifically, and this one does. The reason is that this text assumes a foundation of knowledge by the reader of technical analysis. A simple definition of technical analysis would be the following: the art of attempting to forecast or confirm trends in market price by applying pattern-finding techniques to a set of price history or transformations thereof. While many could argue that the dependence on the past varies from technique to technique, the definition still seems to hold.

Because this chapter assumes at least an elementary understanding of the more popular techniques, it will not try to teach the basics of technical analysis. In referring to "technical analysis," we include in that term indicators (trend following, overbought-oversold, momentum, and volatility-based) as well as charting techniques (chart patterns, trendlines, etc.). Specific versions of any of these will be explained only in their relation to the cross-rate markets.

WHAT'S SO DIFFERENT?

Doubtless the first thought in the technician's mind at this point is, "So what's the big deal . . . after all, technicals are technicals no matter what you're trading, soybeans, stocks, or Swiss francs." True, the principles of technical analysis stay relatively constant across markets. But before futures or stock speculators apply their talents toward cross-rate markets, there are few things they must learn. Three characteristics make this situation a little different:

1. Out of all the markets, you can possibly trade, foreign exchange runs the gamut on the varying degrees to which its markets are susceptible to technical analysis.

2. Out of all the exchange rates, cross rates can be the most pleasing and the most bothersome technical markets to trade.

3. Since the focus is on cross rates here, the arena of activity is going to be the 24-hour, cash interbank market.

Cash or futures, foreign exchange markets exhibit some unique characteristics. Someone once said of the wealthy classes, "The rich? They are *different.*" The currencies are different too. One phenomenon that both bank dealers and futures-trading purist have noticed is that when exchange rates trend, they trend big, but when they're flat, they're really flat and can stay that way for a long while. Technical analysts trading the major exchange rates and cross rates have concluded they see less "in between" type periods in the currencies markets than in other markets. This is a valid observation, considering that in commodities like the agricultural and industrial metal markets, there exists an economically justifiable "base" price that forms a low in an industry filled with players either forcing higher or demanding lower prices. The exchange rate for a currency, by contrast, is controlled by a central bank somewhere, whose goal it is to have the currency's value stay near a target level. Drastic deviations from this level usually occur against the bank's wishes, although changes in the perceptions of people in other countries about the bargaining power of that currency as well as broad economic trends can overcome these wishes. The controlling bank will do everything it can to resist sudden or frequent change. In brief, unlike assets or commodities being pushed to highs or lows, the major currencies have a built-in pressure toward maintaining the norm.

On the other hand, if you had traded the Exchange Rate Mechanism (ERM) cross rates for a while, "in between" trends is all you would have seen. The cross rates governed by exchange rate agreements can often be a real "snore." Of course, devaluation may also serve as a real wake-up call. The important thing to remember, regardless of the type of cross rate, is that in these markets applying your mix of technical studies demands more than the conventional optimization and modification that appears to work in other markets. In addition, the "trending-sideways" quality of these markets most aptly applies to the more popular exchange rates such as sterling-mark and mark-yen. The propensity of a particular exchange rate to trend depends on the exchange rate. Most of the ERM exchange rates could rarely be typified as "trending," as the same goes for Korean won and Hong Kong dollars against U.S. dollars, as they are pegged to U.S. currency.

The discussion of technical analysis in this chapter examines several indicators, and the focus should not be on using these specific indicators as a trading model, but to compare the usefulness of technical models in both the futures and cash markets. Because there are relatively few futures on nondollar cross rates, some of the analysis will focus on dollar-based cross rates. Atop everything else, the technician must adjust to the cash market. You may be or may not be disappointed to find this book written largely from a cash market perspective. Regardless of whether you are a futures or cash trader, the cross-rate market is a 24-hour one, and 24-hour markets not only appear, but behave differently from exchange-traded markets.

THE INDICATORS

Generalizations about a particular exchange-rate can create problems. Each currency and each exchange rate in which it is a component can carry a different character. Figures 5–1 through 5–12 offer a 24-hour interbank bar chart of four dollar-based or cross rates. Each is accompanied by three different technical analysis tools. First, a 9- and 18-day moving average is superimposed over the bar chart. Second, a 14 period relative strength index (RSI) is presented along with the bar chart. Finally, a 20 and 5 period stochastic is shown along with the bar chart. Each indicator is presented on a daily basis, while the dollar-mark is also presented on a weekly basis in Figures 5–13 to 5–15. There are many different types of technical tools, and the ones presented here represent only a small sample of those available. These indicators are

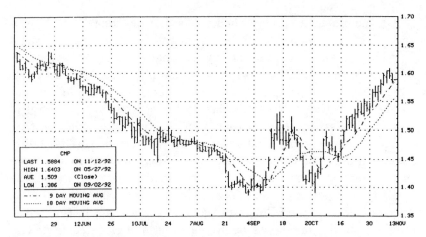

Figure 5–1 Dollar-Mark, Daily Chart from May 12, 1992, to November 12, 1992, with 9- and 18-Day Moving Averages Superimposed on Bar Chart. (*Source:* Bloomberg L.P.)

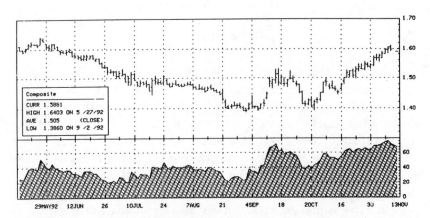

Figure 5–2 Dollar-Mark, Daily Chart from May 12, 1992, to November 12, 1992, with 14-Day RSI. (*Source:* Bloomberg L.P.)

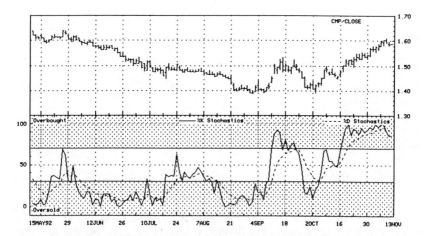

Figure 5–3 Dollar-Mark, Daily Chart from May 12, 1992, to November 12, 1992, with Stochastics. The %*K* line is a 20-day and the %*D* line is a 5-day. Overbought area is shaded above 70%, and oversold area is shaded below 30%. (*Source: Bloomberg L.P.*)

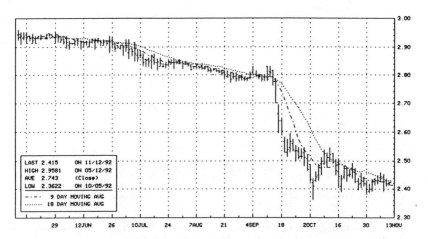

Figure 5–4 Sterling-Mark, Daily Chart from May 12, 1992, to November 12, 1992, with 9- and 18-Day Moving Averages Superimposed on Bar Chart. (*Source: Bloomberg L.P.*)

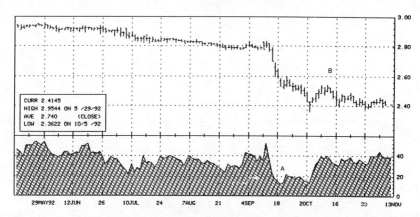

Figure 5–5   Sterling-Mark, Daily Chart from May 12, 1992, to November 12, 1992, with 14-Day RSI. Point A marks an extremely oversold reading on the RSI. Although this traditionally means that the market will rally, the signal was premature. Point B shows a high during a bear market rally, while the corresponding RSI reading is only near 40. This may be a confirmation that the bear market is still intact. (*Source:* Bloomberg L.P.)

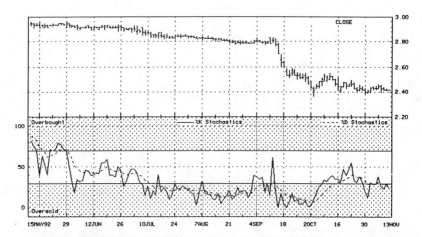

Figure 5–6   Sterling-Mark, Daily Chart from May 12, 1992, to November 12, 1992, with Stochastics. The %K line is a 20-day and the %D line is a 5-day. Overbought area is shaded above 70%, and oversold area is shaded below 30%. (*Source:* Bloomberg L.P.)

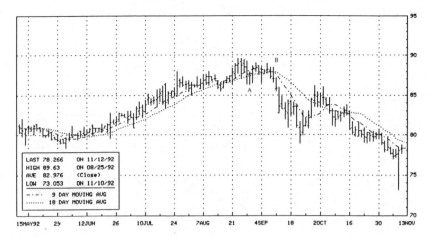

Figure 5–7 Mark-Yen, Daily Chart from May 12, 1992, to November 12, 1992, with 9- and 18-Day Moving Averages Superimposed on Bar Chart. The period of time around point *A* shows many crossovers of price above and below the moving average. At point *B*, there is a crossover in with both the price and the shorter term moving average. (*Source:* Bloomberg L.P.)

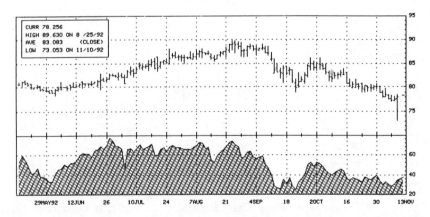

Figure 5–8 Mark-Yen, Daily Chart from May 12, 1992, to November 12, 1992, with 14-Day RSI. (*Source:* Bloomberg L.P.)

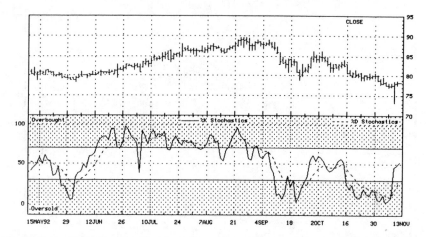

Figure 5–9   Mark-Yen, Daily Chart from May 12, 1992, to November 12, 1992, with Stochastics. The %K line is a 20-day and the %D line is a 5-day. Overbought area is shaded above 70%, and oversold area is shaded below 30%. (*Source: Bloomberg L.P.*)

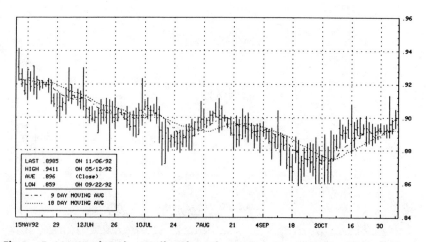

Figure 5–10   Mark-Swiss, Daily Chart from May 12, 1992, to November 12, 1992, with 9- and 18-Day Moving Averages Superimposed on Bar Chart. (*Source: Bloomberg L.P.*)

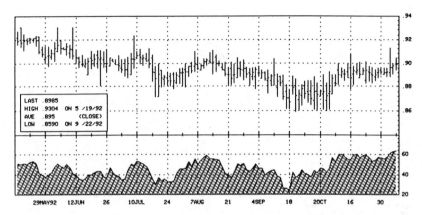

Figure 5–11   Mark-Swiss, Daily Chart from May 12, 1992, to November 12, 1992, with 14-Day RSI. (*Source:* Bloomberg L.P.)

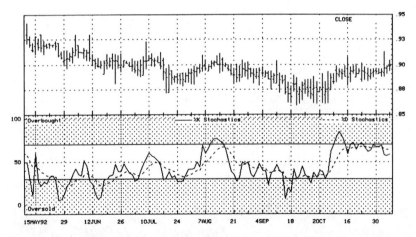

Figure 5–12   Mark-Swiss, Daily Chart from May 12, 1992, to November 12, 1992, with Stochastics. The %*K* line is a 20-day and the %*D* line is a 5-day. Overbought area is shaded above 70%, and oversold area is shaded below 30%. (*Source:* Bloomberg L.P.)

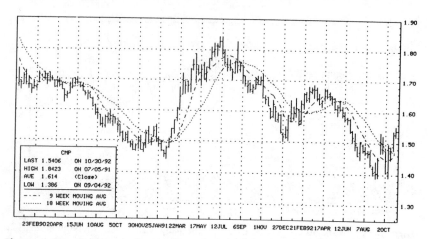

Figure 5–13   Dollar-Mark, Weekly Chart from May 12, 1992, to November 12, 1992, with 9- and 18-Day Moving Averages Superimposed on Bar Chart. (*Source:* Bloomberg L.P.)

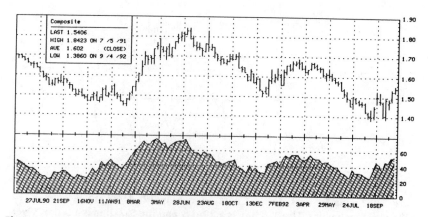

Figure 5–14   Dollar-Mark, Weekly Chart from May 12, 1992, to November 12, 1992, with 14-Day RSI. (*Source:* Bloomberg L.P.)

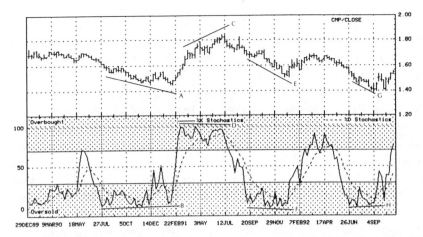

Figure 5–15 Dollar-Mark, Weekly Chart from May 12, 1992, to November 12, 1992, with Stochastics. The %K line is a 20-day and the %D line is a 5-day. Overbought area is shaded above 70%, and oversold area is shaded below 30%. Lines A and B, E, and F, and G and H show bullish divergence, indicating a market low. Lines C and D show bearish divergence, indicating a market high. (Source: Bloomberg L.P.)

presented because they are well known, and have been widely followed in traditional futures markets. In our view, most technical indicators that work in futures will also work in both the cash currency and cross-rate markets. The only caution is that, as discussed earlier, different types of cross rates behave in different ways, and respond differently to technical analysis. For instance, mark-yen behaves very differently from mark-Swiss, and this can be seen in Figures 5–7 and 5–10.

Moving averages are usually regarded as a simple but effective way of measuring whether a market is moving up or down. This makes intuitive sense. If the current price is above its average price for the past 18 days (its 18-day moving average), then it can be said that prices are now high relative to the time period being analyzed. If prices are below the average, then the market is moving lower. As one of the mainstays of early technical analysis, the moving average is considered to be an adequate indicator of trends. On a simple level, we could construct a trading model that would buy if the price went above the moving average and sell when it went below it. Conventional wisdom says that this sort of strategy will catch most long trends, and profit from them. Research has shown that in the past, this has been the case in the currency markets. In each of these figures, with the exception of mark-Swiss, it appears that trading would be profitable for traders who followed the preceding strategy. One reason that the mark-Swiss is not profitable is that the economies of the two countries are so closely related, and trends do not appear over this time horizon.

Another method of trading moving averages that is widely followed is a crossover in the two averages, instead of one of the averages and price. So, a position could be taken when the 9-day average crossed over the 18-day average in the direction of the crossover. This strategy will eliminate some of the false signals but still will catch most of the major moves. An example of this can be seen in Figure 5–7. During the time marked by the letter A, several signals were given by a price crossover model that were reversed the next day. On the other hand, the moving average crossover model maintained a long position in mark-yen throughout. Of course, both methods were able to catch the move lower at point B. In conclusion, the moving average crossover model will eliminate some false signals and catch most major moves, but may not react as fast as the price model. Although these examples are fairly simplistic, they serve to illustrate the use of moving averages in cross rate trading.

The RSI can be interpreted in various ways as well. Some traders adhere to the relatively simple—and mediocre—rule that anything above 75 in the index denotes an overbought market, anything less than 25 means extreme weakness. Others use it for the purpose of divergence with the price chart, for example, the phenomenon of lower lows occurring in price, corresponding with higher lows in the RSI, means a trend change is in the midst. The RSI can also be used as a trend confirmation, employing the rule that an RSI making bottoms and tops between 20 and 60 respectively is associated with an overall bear trend, while those between 40 and 80 confirm a bull trend. A good example of this can be seen in the sterling-mark chart in Figure 5–5. As the market rallied within the context of a bear market, shown by the letter B, the RSI was moving to around 40. This could be used by an astute trader as a point to enter or add to a short position in sterling-mark.

In viewing Figures 5–2, 5–5, 5–8, 5–11, and 5–14, it appears that the RSI can stay at overbought or oversold levels for long periods of time, especially during long trends. Again referring to Figure 5–5, if a short position were covered the first time the RSI has a reading below 25, it would have been much too early, as shown by the letter A on the chart. The lesson here is that RSI can move to overbought or oversold levels early in a trend, and stay there for an extended period of time. Because of this, RSI may best be utilized as a confirmation tool. As with the moving averages earlier, the mark-Swiss does not seem to respond well to RSI analysis.

Stochastics are measurements of short-term movements in price. The theory is that prices tend to close near the upper end of their trading range in uptrends, but as the trend nears its end, there is a tendency for prices to close off of their highs. The reverse is true in down markets. The analysis here is similar to RSI in that high readings are indicative of an overbought market, while low ones mean the market is oversold. Divergence of price and the stochastic indicator also are similar to RSI analysis. In other words, if the price sets a low, and then subsequently sets a lower low, but the stochastic indicator sets a higher low coincidentally with the second price low, a buy signal is generated. The best way to understand this is by looking at an example. Figure 5–15 shows dollar-mark with a stochastic indicator. During the time marked by line *A,* the dollar was setting new lows. However, the stochastic indicator was not setting new lows at the same time, as shown by line *B.* This is divergence and indicates a market low. The reverse of this formation will indicate a market high. Price is setting higher highs, while the stochastic indicator is not. This formation can be seen in Figure 5–15 by lines *C* and *D.* More bullish divergences occur and are indicated by lines *E* and *F,* and *G* and *H.*

Normally, divergences are most easily found in the %K line (solid), but longer term ones can also be found using the %D line (dashed). There are also different formations such as failures and crossovers of the %K and %D lines. Interpreting these formations requires the study of many different markets and market situations, and is beyond the scope of this text, but can be found in most books on technical analysis. As a general statement, stochastics, like the RSI, may also be used for trading filters and trend confirmation indicators, and seem to work reasonably well when applied to the cash cross-rate markets.

The character of a particular exchange rate also includes some description of its volatility or propensity to trend. One indicator designed to measure trendiness is the Average Directional Index (ADX), originally introduced by Welles Wilder. The ADX attempts to measure the trendiness of a market. By tracking the degree of deviations from some norm, or average of closing prices over a given period, the ADX appears to serve as a nice record of past movement of the exchange rate. On an ADX chart, the higher the number, the stronger the current trend—

bull or bear. The ADX is measured by a scale between zero and about 50, with the higher reading meaning a stronger trend.

Since the ADX was first charted, traders have explored how to implement it as a trading filter. The basic idea is to have something that says, "Ignore that moving average crossover, the market is not trending now." The traditional rule-of-thumb for applying the ADX in this way has been to pay more attention to trading signals that occur as the line is rising between 18 and 25. As with any indicator, using the ADX as a trend indicator is subject to experimentation and interpretation. You can follow daily or weekly versions, but to serve as a filter the daily indicator makes more sense. One approach would be to give more weight to trading signals that occur when the ADX is between 10 and 25 and rising. Figures 5–16 through 5–18 show this in mark-yen. The cross rate is

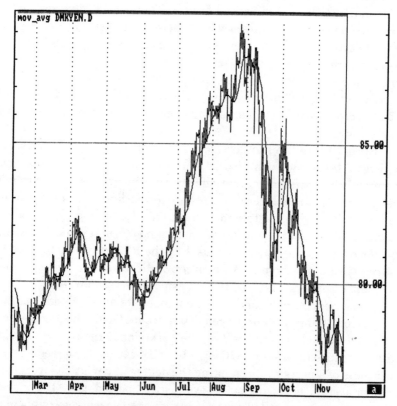

Figure 5–16   Mark-Yen, Daily Chart from April 1992 to November 1992, with 9-Day Moving Average Superimposed on Bar Chart. (*Source:* Telerate)

shown with a superimposed moving average and is followed by a 9-day and 18-day ADX. Note how the shorter term version not only drops sooner but begins to signal strength in the new trend earlier. Others have employed alternative means of determining whether a market is "trendy" or not, such as implied volatility from the corresponding options market. Yet the ADX remains one of the most popular.

Trendiness indicators, like the ADX, are the source of much debate. Like most indicators that help make sense of the past, they can be dangerous for the future. Currency traders can apply this type of study to learn how a market begins a trend, continues the trend, and

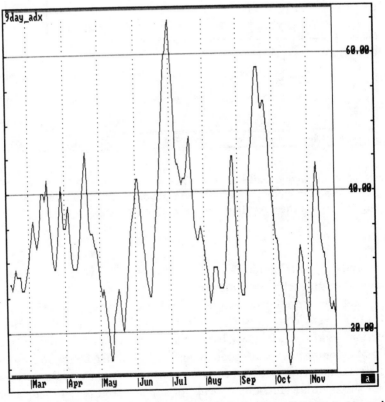

Figure 5–17   Mark-Yen, Daily 9-Day ADX Chart from April 1992 to November 1992. This is an example of a short-term trendiness indicator. The higher the reading, the greater the strength of the trend. (*Source:* Telerate)

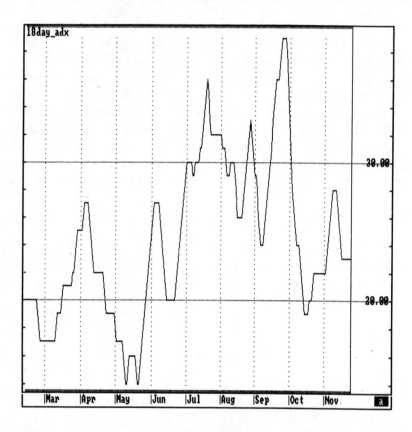

Figure 5–18 Mark-Yen, Daily 18-Day ADX Chart from April 1992 to November 1992. This is an example of a medium-term trendiness indicator. The higher the reading, the greater the strength of the trend. (*Source:* Telerate)

then turns or travels sideways. Such analyses are very important in trading foreign exchange markets.

Another common method of technical analysis is charting. This type of analysis looks at patterns in prices to determine their future direction. Again, since entire books have been written on patterns, we will not attempt to explain their usage here, but use a simple example to differentiate the case and futures markets. This example will center on the popular charting concept of support and resistance, which holds that if a market has set an important high or low, and prices return to those levels, they will have some difficulty moving through them. This is evidenced on a chart by a double-top or double-bottom formation. These patterns seem to present themselves in both dollar-based and cross-rate markets fairly frequently. For traders interested in long-term charts, the major cash cross rates are presented from 1980 to 1992 in the Appendix, courtesy of Datastream International. A very interesting question arises, however, when comparing the cash and futures markets. Which market should a trader look to in establishing support and resistance levels? This question becomes important because of the possibility (which has happened often) that the two markets will give conflicting signals.

For example, suppose the cash market in dollar-mark sets a low, and then rallies off it, and the futures market does the same. When that low is retested at a later date, the futures market may go through it. Remember, of course, that the futures will be setting new highs because the futures are priced in currency while the cash market is priced in dollars. Because the futures market reflects the cash market plus or minus the interest rate carry charge to the futures expiration date, the cash and futures prices may not be at exactly the same level as they were at the previous low. As clarification, let's assume that the dollar returns to a point just *above* its previous low against the mark, as shown in Figures 5–19 and 5–20 of the cash and futures markets. Because of the interest rate carry cost, the D-mark futures on the IMM

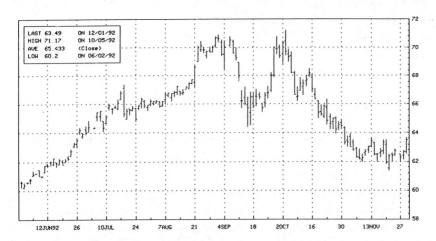

Figure 5–19 December D-Mark, Daily Chart from June 1, 1992, to December 1, 1992. Notice the high set around the first of September, and the next high around the first of October. The October high was a new high. This may be viewed as a breakout and as bearish for the dollar. (*Source:* Bloomberg L.P.)

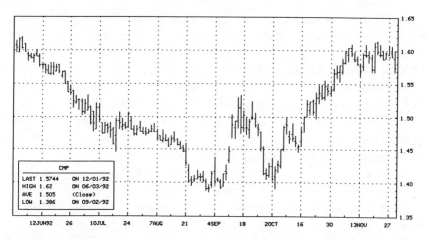

Figure 5–20   Dollar-Mark, Daily Chart from June 1, 1992, to December 1, 1992.
Notice the low set around the first of September, and the next low around the first
of October. The October low was not a new low. This may be viewed as a failure to
set new lows and as bullish for the dollar. (*Source:* Bloomberg L.P.)

has just set a new high. Is this a breakout or a failure? It is a breakout
in the futures market, but a failure in the cash market. Trading experience has shown that the cash market is the important one to watch. In
this example, the odds are that dollar-mark would rally from this point.
Interestingly enough, on an intraday basis, the futures market will often lead the cash market, but on a long-term basis, the cash market will
usually be the leader.

ANALYZING FIXED EXCHANGE-RATE SYSTEMS

In Chapter 1, we introduced several different categories of cross rates,
and showed how these categories are distinguished. An exchange rate
can exist between trading partners, between members of a exchange-
rate agreement, between high- and low-yielding currencies, or include
an exotic currency. Each sort of cross rate exhibits unique characteristics. This section focuses on the second genre mentioned: exploring the
rules to use for exchange rates guided by government policy or express
treaty, such as the ERM.

Most importantly, the exchange rates between members of mechanisms like the ERM offer technical analysts a unique perspective.

At first glance, the regulated trading ranges between the European currencies in the ERM would seem to constitute a technician's dream—steady support and resistance boundaries that indicate when the currency might be too strong or too weak and due for a correction.

For the technical analyst, the question remains whether there exists any advantage to the presence of these trading zones, and how exactly does the trader use these exchange-rate boundaries to advantageously. Figure 5–21 exhibits daily movements of a prominent ERM cross rate, the sterling-mark from early 1992.

As you can see by the chart, even though sterling was forced to abide by strict intervention limits, it still enjoys a great deal of latitude against the D-mark. However, thinking of the ERM exchange rates as an excellent range-trading market may oversimplify matters. In fact, there are a number of twists in an ERM cross rate that should be understood before actually trading. Most important for traders to remember is how the ERM, and the European Monetary System (EMS) in general, works. As explained in Chapter 3, each ERM currency must abide by a mid-range or "parity" value, an upper limit, and a lower limit against a basket of all the ERM currencies structured around the D-mark.

There are also limits against the Ecu but they serve merely as a theoretical backdrop for the workings of the ERM. In practice, the limits

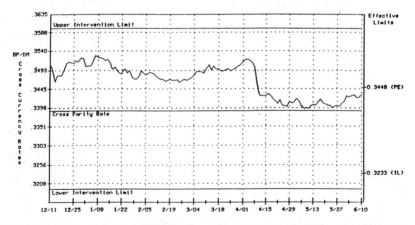

Figure 5–21　Sterling-Mark, from December 1991 to June 1992, with Cross Parity Rate, Upper Intervention Limit, and Lower Intervention Limit. Also shown on the right side of the chart is the implied ceiling, against the Portuguese escudo (PE), and the implied floor, against the Italian lira (IL). (*Source:* Bloomberg L.P.)

against the Ecu are usually maintained, but only incidentally, as the central banks of the ERM countries pay more attention to what their currency is doing against the D-mark. Each ERM currency must also abide by intervention bands against all other ERM currencies. While the German currency was supposed to be just another currency in this vein, it has taken on the role of a surrogate Ecu.

This introduces what is perhaps the more important rule for the ERM currencies. Technicians adamant about treating the ERM cross rates as trading range markets should forget about the intervention limits and concentrate on "implied floors." Even a depreciating currency that is nowhere near its lower intervention band against the D-mark (or Ecu) may still find itself at its lowest limit against a *third* currency in the system. This concept of the implied floor of an ERM currency can be difficult to understand at first glance. A simple way of looking at implied floors is that the floor is the lowest cross rate one currency may trade at relative to another and still be above the prescribed limit. To illustrate, let us look back at the spring 1992 adjustments in interest rates that affected the exchange rate between the D-mark and the Spanish peseta. At that time, the British pound was trading at the lower end of its band against the Spanish currency, while the peseta was trading near or at its *upper* boundary with respect to the D-mark. In essence, the peseta's knocking against its all-important ceiling with the D-mark meant the pound was "locked up" against not only the peseta but other currencies as well. Thus, the Bank of England and others wanted to see the pound fall, but because it could not drop against the peseta, it couldn't against the others as well. However, Spanish interest rates were lowered to bring the peseta down relative to the mark. The change in Spanish rates not only accomplished its goal, but allowed sterling to fall relative to the mark. Astute traders may be able to take advantage of these movements to profit by trading cross rates.

Figures 5–22 through 5–30 help illustrate the force of intervention bands and implied floors, as well as what tends to happen to currencies that stray from their appointed parity values with the D-mark. These charts are for the time period leading up to mid-1992. The upper- and lower-bands and the parity values against the D-mark run across each chart.

The divergence indicator in Figure 5–26 is Bloomberg System's version of a caution signal for detecting ERM currencies that are moving out of line. The vendor calculates the indicator based on the currency's deviation from parity with the Ecu or D-mark. The deviation

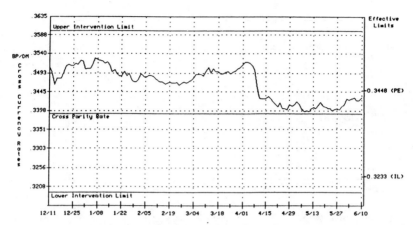

Figure 5–22 **Sterling-Mark, from December 1991 to June 1992, with Cross Parity Rate, Upper Intervention Limit, and Lower Intervention Limit. Also shown on the right side of the chart is the implied ceiling, against the Portuguese escudo (PE), and the implied floor, against the Italian lira (IL). (*Source:* Bloomberg L.P.)**

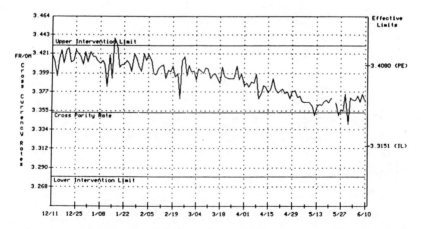

Figure 5–23 **Mark-French, from December 1991 to June 1992, with Cross Parity Rate, Upper Intervention Limit, and Lower Intervention Limit. Also shown on the right side of the chart is the implied ceiling, against the Portuguese escudo (PE), and the implied floor, against the Italian lira (IL). (*Source:* Bloomberg L.P.)**

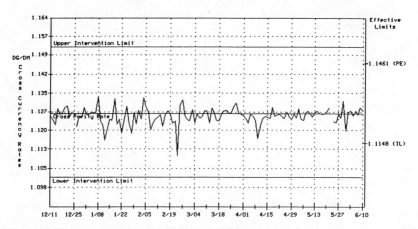

Figure 5–24 Mark-Guilder, from December 1991 to June 1992, with Cross Parity Rate, Upper Intervention Limit, and Lower Intervention Limit. Also shown on the right side of the chart is the implied ceiling, against the Portuguese escudo (PE), and the implied floor, against the Italian lira (IL). (*Source:* Bloomberg L.P.)

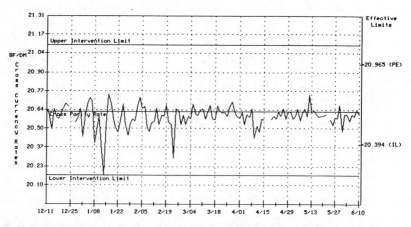

Figure 5–25 Mark-Belgian Franc, from December 1991 to June 1992, with Cross Parity Rate, Upper Intervention Limit, and Lower Intervention Limit. Also shown on the right side of the chart is the implied ceiling, against the Portuguese escudo (PE), and the implied floor, against the Italian lira (IL). (*Source:* Bloomberg L.P.)

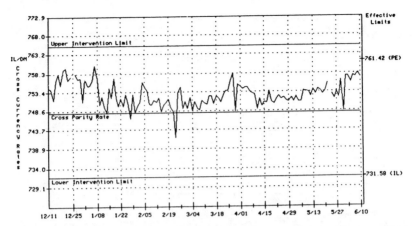

Figure 5–26 **Mark-Lira, from December 1991 to June 1992, with Cross Parity Rate, Upper Intervention Limit and Lower Intervention Limit. Also shown on the right side of the chart is the implied ceiling, against the Portuguese escudo (PE), and the implied floor, against the Italian lira (IL). (Source: Bloomberg L.P.)**

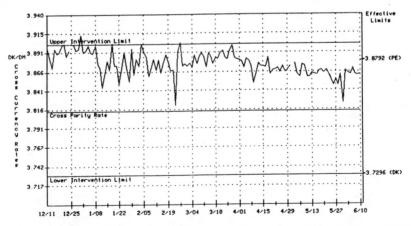

Figure 5–27 **Mark-Krone, from December 1991 to June 1992, with Cross Parity Rate, Upper Intervention Limit, and Lower Intervention Limit. Also shown on the right side of the chart is the implied ceiling, against the Portuguese escudo (PE), and the implied floor, against the Danish krone (DK). (Source: Bloomberg L.P.)**

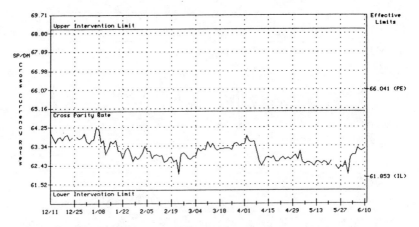

Figure 5–28 Mark-Peseta, from December 1991 to June 1992, with Cross Parity Rate, Upper Intervention Limit, and Lower Intervention Limit. Also shown on the right side of the chart is the implied ceiling, against the Portuguese escudo (PE), and the implied floor, against the Italian lira (IL). (*Source:* Bloomberg L.P.)

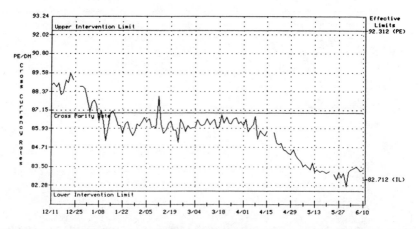

Figure 5–29 Mark-Escudo, from December 1991 to June 1992, with Cross Parity Rate, Upper Intervention Limit, and Lower Intervention Limit. Also shown on the right side of the chart is the implied ceiling, against the Portuguese escudo (PE), and the implied floor, against the Italian lira (IL). (*Source:* Bloomberg L.P.)

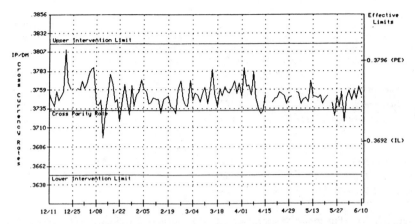

Figure 5–30 Mark-Irish Pound, from December 1991 to June 1992, with Cross Parity Rate, Upper Intervention Limit, and Lower Intervention Limit. Also shown on the right side of the chart is the implied ceiling, against the Portuguese escudo (PE), and the implied floor, against the Italian lira (IL). (*Source:* Bloomberg L.P.)

is then adjusted by the relative weight of the currency in composing the Ecu.

Because the D-mark, for example, makes up just less than one-third of the Ecu, compared with the Portuguese escudo, which constitutes much less, deviations of the same size in both—without adjustment—would seem much greater for the escudo. The divergence indicator was originally intended to function as an early warning signal. The indicator also assumes each currency abides by a 2.25% deviation band. In more precise terms, as of summer 1992, the indicator was calculated in the following manner: (1) the percentage deviation from parity with the Ecu is determined; (2) since the percentage deviation assumes 2.25% intervention bands, it must be adjusted for the effect on the Ecu by the three currencies that are allowed to stray 6.0% (the peseta, the escudo, and the pound); (3) Bloomberg calculates the "maximum divergence spread" as the maximum allowable deviation (2.25% or 6.0%) weighted by the currency's weight in the basket. (For example, for the French franc, with a 19.3% weight in the basket, the maximum divergence spread is $(1 - 0.193) \times 2.25\% = 1.916\%$.); (4) finally, the ratio of the adjusted percentage deviation (2) to the maximum divergence spread (3) is expressed as a percentage to obtain the divergence indicator (see Figure 5–31).

CURRENCY (Direct)	SPOT vs DM	PARITY vs DM	% DEV. FROM DM PARITY	% DEV. FROM DM	DIVERGENCE INDICATOR
1) Portugese Escudo	83.22	86.94	4.278	4.278	77
2) Spanish Peseta	63.17	65.00	2.822	2.822	55
3) Belgian Franc	20.62	20.63	0.016	0.016	21
4) Netherlands Guilder	1.126	1.127	0.028	0.028	16
5) German Deutschemark	1.000	1.000			19
6) Irish Punt	0.3748	0.3733	−0.417	−0.417	−4
7) French Franc	3.368	3.354	−0.409	−0.409	−6
8) Italian Lira	756.4	748.2	−1.096	−1.096	−41
9) British Pound	0.3430	0.3390	−1.198	−1.198	−15
10) Danish Krone	3.854	3.814	−1.045	−1.045	−42

Figure 5–31 European Monetary System Divergence Indicator. The levels were calculated on June 11, 1992. (*Source:* Bloomberg L.P.)

INTERMARKET ANALYSIS

If you are an international bond trader, you've probably heard that breakouts in the crude oil market have long been thought to foreshadow similar breakouts—in the opposite direction—in the Japanese bond market. If you are a stock analyst, you're more than likely tuned in to how different industry groups interact and the lag time in their respective moves. An "intermarket" approach to a particular market, simply put, is the practice of employing the activity or forecasts for one market as an input for the forecasting of another. This is a realm ruled by chartists and statisticians. This practice has already been touched on twice in the previous sections: using a cash versus futures chart comparison, and contrasting individual ERM rates against the Ecu.

Until now, this chapter has focused on technical analysis of the cross rate itself. Intermarket study employs the analysis of other rates and other markets. The currency markets seem almost tailor-made for intermarket analysis. In the bond trader's case, the connection between crude oil and the Japanese credit markets is intuitively economic: Higher petroleum prices will translate to greater inflation in oil-scarce Japan. In currencies, a similar relationship exists between the exchange rates and interest rates. Currency traders also enjoy a much more close-knit form of intermarket relationships. Currency could be viewed as a stand-alone "asset," but the truth is currencies only have meaning when expressed in terms of another currency. It is this quality that makes the foreign exchange market special: Intermarket relationships are important because the market itself exists as an array of intermarket relationships.

Analysis of markets by way of other markets may be a discipline that comes easier to non-U.S.-based traders. While many U.S. precious metals dealers have gotten used to tracking the price of gold in Japanese yen, how many Swiss franc traders down on the floor of the Chicago Merc continuously track the currency's value in D-marks? Even in determining the trend of the Swiss franc against the U.S.dollar, the European foreign exchange dealer stays glued to the mark-Swiss market. Only recently have many currency traders discovered just how important it is to know what dollar-sterling is doing in order to figure out dollar-mark. Stock analysts may talk of the U.S. government bond market, and oil traders may keep an eye on the price of gold, yet those markets all remain in their own separate networks. In the interbank market, the trader can change from quotes on mark-yen to those for Swiss-yen then to the spread on Swiss-peseta without taking a breath. In the futures markets, traders speculate on spreads between different—sometimes remote—markets. Take the spread between Treasury note futures and Treasury Bond futures, otherwise known as the "NOB" spread. The connection between the spread market and the T-note and T-bond markets is mathematical and is a function of the steepness of the yield curve. A large move in one of the markets must automatically spell a thinning or widening of the spread. Therefore, a trader who can forecast a move in one of the legs of the spread, can also forecast the spread itself.

Similarly, cross-rate traders have the ability to analyze markets in a unique way by using intermarket analysis. The difference between this and the previous example in the bond market is that there is not necessarily a mathematical relationship. The true value of intermarket analysis in currencies and cross rates is that often a change in a cross rate can signal an upcoming change in a dollar-based currency, and vice versa. In other words, one can be used as confirmation of the other. An excellent example of this is found in Figures 5–32 and 5–33. In late August 1992, the mark-yen cross put in a high (Figure 5–32). The question at this time was whether or not this was a significant market turning point, or just a brief respite. Confirmation of the high can be found in Figure 5–33, in which the dollar bottoms at about the same time.

This example may seem obvious since both figures show the same thing, mark weakness. Although this is true, there is still validity in this type of analysis. We have seen many instances where the end of a

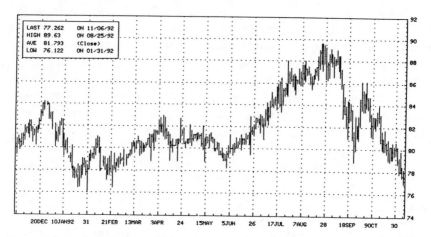

Figure 5-32 Mark-Yen, Daily Chart from November 29, 1991, to November 6, 1992. (*Source:* Bloomberg L.P.)

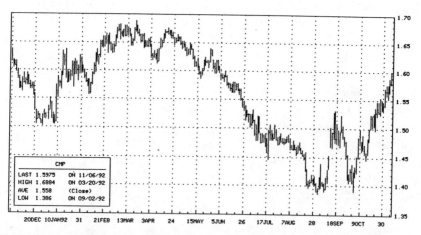

Figure 5-33 Dollar-Mark, Daily Chart from November 29, 1991, to November 6, 1992. The highs and lows can be compared with the mark-yen chart in Figure 5-32 to confirm major turning points. (*Source:* Bloomberg L.P.)

long sustained trend in one market was signaled one to two days in advance by another. This sort of analysis can be a powerful tool, and is uniquely suited to the cross-rate markets.

APPLYING YOUR SYSTEM TO THE CASH MARKET

Traders who rely on technical analysis tend to become systemized. Usually, to be successful, they must consult their studies and indicators, and chart patterns in a consistent manner. Technical analysis also lends itself well to the trading system, a mechanical approach to the market that yields buy and sell signals. Many technically oriented traders of varying backgrounds eventually give in to the temptation of building a trading system. For those traders in the futures markets who now want to trade cash, an interesting question arises: Can they take their reliable futures-trading systems into the cash with them? Earlier, we explored the differences between the two realms. The same cash market that lured in the trader with promises of new bounty in additional and exotic currencies and cross rates is also a 24-hour one, offering no official "open" and "close" and no volume or open interest figures to speak of. At least some of these data are necessary for both technical analysis and trading systems to work.

Technicians in the cash market have two choices: (1) keep applying their system solely to the futures market and—when a signal is emitted—act on it in the cash market; (2) tailor the system and its inputs to adapt to the cash market. Many traders, including some successful trading advisors, are opting for the former plan. They still perform their analysis on futures prices and trade their signals in the cash. Yet, this seems intuitively counterproductive: Why take positions in a deep and virtually unlimited market (cash) when the analysis is based on mere bits and pieces of a duplicate market? Tailoring technical studies to the cash market may be the most logical answer. In truth, unless the studies incorporate daily trading volume or some other figure not obtainable in the cash market, the indicator formula itself is fine. The price data are what require tailoring. Most technical trading systems must somehow cope with the reality of a market without any open or close, let alone high or low. One way to alleviate this problem is to call arbitrarily designate one point in the 24-hour period as the "open" and another as the "close," monitoring the high and low that occurs in between.

Traders could create an entire industry around the manipulation of 24-hour cash data before technicals are even applied. Fans of optimization and statistical research have already embarked on this process. One decision that has probably already been made is the preference for daily or intraday price data. Intraday traders actually have it easier, as five minutes in the futures markets are still equal to that in cash. As for daily-based traders, many have taken the approach suggested earlier and simply marked an "open" somewhere and a "close" somewhere else. The solution employed by one of the authors involves creating a daily bar that covers the most active period of the world's trading. This period could begin at the open in Sydney—the first market to open in the Far East—and end with the close in New York. Such a period constitutes a 24-hour open-high-low-close bar that does a fairly good job of tracking daily price movements in the cash currency markets.

The reason for creating the 24-hour bar is to test systems using cash data, the obvious difference being the potential for different high-to-low price ranges. Taking this one step further, assume that a trader is designing a trading system for the cash market, but tests it on the futures market. How will he know if his stops are being hit overnight? He won't. The cash market may, and often does, move outside the daily ranges of the futures markets, and this could impact the system test. The trader must solve this problem before he can really trust his results. Another problem is that the markets do not have the same liquidity all night. For, instance dollar-mark trades more actively in Europe and the United States than it does in the Far East, so there is a question as to the relative importance of the price data from each trading center. Figure 5–34 is a good representation of the trading activity throughout a typical 24-hour day.

Other traders have taken more creative approaches. One currency chartist has encouraged slicing the around-the-clock trading into several portions. Anyone who has ever seen a bar chart is familiar with this concept. A trading day in any market can be chopped into portions representing an hour or a number of minutes worth of trading. Some chartists have suggested taking a trading day and slicing it into two, three, or even four equal units, each with its own high, low, open, and close. However, novelty has its limits—dividing up the day any more than this gets you right back to the hourly bar.

Some productive research has been done in breaking the day down into three periods: one when markets are open in the Far East, one when they are open in Europe, and one for U.S. trading hours.

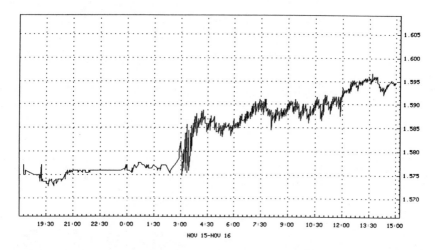

Figure 5–34 Dollar-Mark, Intraday Chart from November 15/16, 1992. The heavier the trading, the more dense the line. Trading can be very light in the Far East, and then pick up during European and U.S. hours. The times shown at the bottom are Eastern Standard times. (*Source:* Bloomberg L.P.)

The theory here is that signals based on yen-dominated currency rates would react more, and give more reliable signals if they were based on Far East trading alone, or at least if these data were given more weight. Similarly, European-based crosses should be tracked in Europe; and dollar-based crosses, in the United States. The problem with this analysis is twofold. First, how do you deal with interregion cross rates such as mark-yen? Second, there is an overlap of European and U.S. trading hours. (This is not a problem in the Far East since those hours do not overlap with either Europe or the United States.) However, as a result, this methodology has achieved only limited success at this time.

6

BRINGING IT ALL TOGETHER—SPECIFIC STRATEGIES AND TACTICS

In this chapter, we will deal with specific tactics and methodology for utilizing the cash currency market, and more specifically the cross-rate markets, to develop trading strategies. This chapter is not intended to be a summary. Many strategies and tactics have already been suggested elsewhere in the text. We will first examine fixed exchange rate systems by using the European Exchange Rate Mechanism (ERM) as an example. Next, we will look at trading realignments within a fixed-rate system, again using the ERM as an example. We will then leave the arena of fixed exchange rate systems and move toward other types of market strategies. These will focus on currency ranking models and triangular trading. Finally, the discussion will consider the process of adding cross-rate trading to an existing trading system.

TRADING FIXED-RATE SYSTEMS

The basic guidelines for trading the ERM currencies were laid out in Chapters 3 and 5. One point made clear was the appearance of the

ERM currencies as formidable "trading range" markets. However, there is also the omnipresent possibility that the currencies will be realigned. Realignments can be profitable trading opportunities or can cause substantial losses depending on the position. Generally, when a currency is near its limit against another within the grid, the adjustment will take the form of either a realignment or interest rate adjustment. Analysis can be done to determine which will occur. Generally this analysis centers around the political impact of interest rate movements on the home economy or the negative impact of a currency devaluation. A realignment will usually occur relative to the D-mark, since it is the dominant currency within the EMS grid.

From a trading standpoint, money can be made three ways within the ERM markets: (1) as an interest rate play, (2) as speculation on exchange rate move, or (3) as a combination of these two. The first situation can occur when the trader does not expect the cross-rate relationship to change. In this case the trader may buy the currency with the higher interest rate and sell the lower yielding one. This generates a positive cost of carry, and the trader will earn the difference between the two rates. For example, if the British pound is yielding more than the French franc, a trader could buy the pound and earn British interest rates, while simultaneously selling the franc and paying out French rates, which would give a positive carry. Unfortunately, the cross rate rarely remains constant over time. While the trader is trying to earn the 3% interest rate differential, the pound could fall by 5% against the franc, and all the profit would be lost. This illustrates the fundamental link between interest rates and foreign exchange.

The yield curves in each market are linked through the forward foreign exchange market. This is because foreign exchange transactions are actually the exchange of two series of future cash flows, in effect a swap. Thus the forward rate is a function of the spot rate and the interest rate differential. This can be expressed mathematically as follows:

$$FR = SR \times ((1 + ix)/(1 + iy))$$

where

$$FR = \text{forward exchange rate}$$
$$SR = \text{spot exchange rate}$$
$$ix = \text{interest rate in currency } x$$
$$iy = \text{interest rate in currency } y$$

If the balance implied by this equation does not hold true, a mispricing in the forward or cash market and an arbitrage opportunity would appear to exist. In reality, there are so many market participants, and the market is so efficient, that these arbitrage opportunities almost never exist for anyone but bank dealers.

Second, a trader who expects movement of one currency within the grid may trade it to capture the price move. For example, if conditions in Italy were such that the lira was expected to fall versus the mark, the trader could sell lira and buy marks. Before doing any further analysis, the trader must be aware that the best situation is when there is a wide interest rate differential between the two currencies and the currencies are near the outer limits of their range. In a situation where a currency is near its upper or lower EMS boundary, the trader must be relatively confident that the adjustment will not be made through realignment. The currency may then be bought or sold in anticipation of central bank intervention.

The third and most ideal way to trade the EMS currencies is to combine the two previous strategies. In other words, if a currency is trading near the low end of its band against another currency and had a positive carry, profits can be made from both an interest rate capture and a currency move. An example of this would be if the Spanish peseta were trading near the low end of its band with the D-mark. At this writing, the peseta is paying a higher interest rate than the mark, so the trader is effectively receiving peseta rates while paying out mark rates, thus earning a positive carry of several percentage points. As long as there was not a realignment of the band, the trader could also profit by holding this cross rate as the central banks of both countries intervened in the markets to buy pesetas and sell marks.

In conclusion, a fixed exchange rate system can be a very profitable environment for range trading. You may refer back to Chapter 5 (Figures 5–21 through 5–30) for an example. The range trader could simply buy the currency whenever it approached its implied floor, or sell it when it neared its ceiling. If the trade had the added benefit of being a positive carry trade, so much the better. The central banks of the world are on the trader's side, and the money comes easy. If this environment exists in the future, it will be a profitable way for traders to be positioned in the market.

TRADING REALIGNMENTS

Before you rush out and start trading in fixed exchange rate systems, we should examine the downside—realignment. A stark example can be seen in comparing the mark-peseta cross from early summer in 1992, with the same cross rate in late 1992 (Figures 6–1 and 6–2). The peseta is still trading within its intervention limits. But the real killer is that the intervention limits have been changed. This is the reality of realignment.

The real test for traders in fixed exchange rate systems is whether or not they can spot the realignment coming. We will examine the realignment in the ERM in September 1992 as an example, and use England as a specific case. It is always easy to say in retrospect that the move was obvious, but to see it in advance is actually fairly difficult. In fact, it may be easier to see from a distant vantage point. This appears to be the case in this example, because the majority of Europeans were convinced that the pound would hold up against the mark, even at the very end. On the other hand, it seems that most of the money was made by non-Europeans who saw the breakup coming, and took large short positions in sterling-mark in both the cash and OTC options markets.

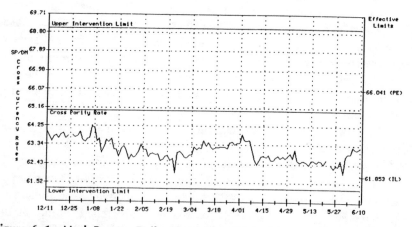

Figure 6–1 Mark-Peseta, Daily Chart from December 11, 1991, to June 10, 1992, with Cross Parity Rate, Upper Intervention Limit, and Lower Intervention Limit. Also shown on the right side of the chart is the implied ceiling, against the Portuguese escudo (PE), and the implied floor, against the Italian lira (IL). (*Source:* Bloomberg L.P.)

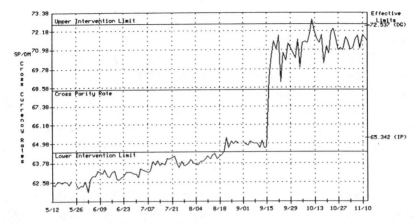

Figure 6-2   Mark-Peseta, Daily Chart from May 12, 1992, to November 10, 1992, with Cross Parity Rate, Upper Intervention Limit, and Lower Intervention Limit. Also shown on the right side of the chart is the implied ceiling, against the Dutch guilder (DG), and the implied floor, against the Irish pound (IP). This is the same cross rate as in Figure 6–1, but at a later date. Notice what happens to the cross rate when there is a devaluation. Also compare the cross parity rates and intervention limits from this chart with those in Figure 6–1. They have been adjusted because of the devaluation. (*Source:* Bloomberg L.P.)

As background, the pound had been near its ERM floor of about 2.80 DM/BP in the spring, as it appeared that the ruling Conservative party was going to lose the general election to the anti-business Labour party. The Conservatives pulled off a huge surprise victory, and the pound rallied back to its central parity level as euphoria swept the British financial markets. This did not last long, though, as disenchantment with the government's inability to get the economy going coupled with no real new ideas, forced the pound back to near its lows.

Meanwhile, Germany was keeping its interest rates high to help keep off inflationary pressures from several fronts, including the assimilation of eastern Germany. The Bundesbank is not a political body and was keeping interest rates high even though there was tremendous pressure from their European neighbors to lower them. Other countries were not able to lower their interest rates because capital would flow out, and into the higher paying mark. So, as summer progressed, most of the European currencies were trading near their floors against the mark.

Even though the British politicians had seemed to stake their political careers on defending the pound, they were forced to devalue the currency because they were unwilling to continue to keep interest rates high and risk a worsening economy. The pound immediately fell by about 15% before it stabilized, and the British were able to lower their interest rates without fear of hurting the currency; it had already been effectively devalued (Figure 6–3).

So, could a trader have seen this coming? Many did and were able to capture enormous profits. It should be instructional to examine another country that was able to effectively defend its currency during the same time, and contrast it with the pound. This currency, which came under extreme selling pressure, but did not devalue was the Swedish krona. This discussion should also help future traders of a fixed exchange system better understand the risks. The single biggest difference between England and Sweden was Sweden's ability to raise interest rates, at whatever the cost. In England, it was politically impossible to raise interest rates to defend the pound. The economy was in the midst of a recession, and neither the people or the government had the stomach to see higher interest rates grind the economy to a halt. On the other hand, the Swedish government was in a much better position to raise rates and defend the currency. As pressure came on the krona, rates started to edge up to 14%, then 18% and then 24%. Suddenly, a run on the currency was on. Interest rates were raised again and the speculators who were betting on a devaluation and had shorted the

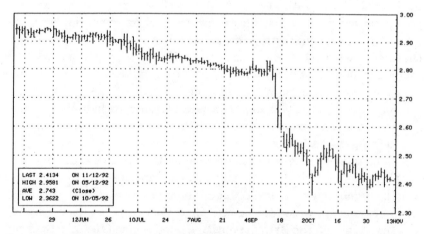

Figure 6–3 Sterling-Mark, Daily Chart from May 13, 1992, to November 12, 1992. This shows the huge drop in the cross rate during devaluation. (*Source:* Bloomberg L.P.)

krona against the mark were now facing interest rates of 500%. It takes a very daring trader to take a trade with that high of a negative carry: Remember, the seller of krona must pay out Swedish short-term rates to maintain the short position. The tactic worked, and the krona was able to stave off devaluation, at least in the short term. The lesson to be learned from all of this is that the political side of the equation must be closely examined. If a trader questions whether or not the government will be able to defend its currency, either because of political pressure or shortages of money (the government may spend huge amounts to defend its currency), then the trader should be extremely careful in trading fixed exchange systems.

CURRENCY RANKING MODELS

Although trading fixed exchange systems from either a trading range perspective or by speculating on realignment can be both exciting and profitable, there are other ways to trade cross rates. In fact, most of the major cash currency rates as well as the exotic ones are not part of a fixed system. So that leaves the trader in need of other ways to trade cross rates. In this section, simple currency ranking models will be discussed.

To understand this type of analysis, it is first necessary to discuss the basis for ranking models. Ranking models focus on currencies, not exchange rates. On a basic level, an analyst will make a list of currencies putting the stronger ones at the top of the list, and those expected to do poorly at the bottom. There are many ways to rank the cross rates, but the most widely used center on interest rate analysis or technical analysis.

Ranking cross rates based on interest rate levels makes some intuitive sense. If current interest rates are high in a particular country, that currency should attract capital as a result. In addition, expectations for rates may play an important role in the pricing of the cross rate, as will the interest rates in other countries. Going back to our European examples, not only are interest rates in England important, but so are expectations of future rates, as well as the rates of other countries in Europe, and to a certain extent, those in the United States.

Thus, to set up a cross-rate-ranking model using interest rates as a base for analysis, a trader could analyze a group of currencies against each other and create cross rates from the combination. Each of these cross rates could then be ranked according to their prospects of appreciation. A trading strategy would then be simply to buy those at the top of the list and sell the ones at the bottom. This may be an oversimplification, but it serves as a good conceptual example. Of course, there are dangers as well in trading in this manner. Before starting to rank currencies, the trader should be aware that there will be a bias towards nondiversification. In other words, assume that a trader ranks 10 currencies against each other, forming a group of cross rates based on interest rate assumptions and analysis of the respective yield curves. The trader then buys the top three ranked cross rates and sell the bottom three. The reality is that, because of this analysis, one currency is ranked highly, and another is low. Therefore, the three cross rates the trader buys may all have the same strong currency underlying them, and the three sold will all have the weak one as a base. The result is a bias toward the two currencies, and no real diversification is achieved. The trader might have been just as well off to trade only the cross between the strongest and weakest currency, instead of incurring transaction costs for all six. Successful traders using ranking models know this and have sophisticated methods of achieving proper diversification.

Another ranking method for trading cross rates could be more geared toward technical analysis. For example, the same cross rates

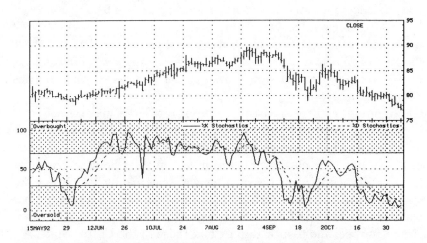

Figure 6–4 Mark-Yen, Daily Chart from May 13, 1992, to November 6, 1992, with Stochastics. The %K line is a 20-day and the %D line is a 5-day. The shaded area marked overbought is above 70%, while the shaded oversold area is below 30%. Higher readings show more strength. (*Source:* Bloomberg L.P.)

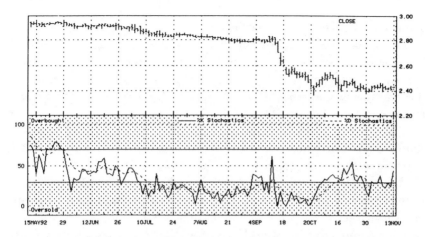

Figure 6–5   Sterling-Mark, Daily Chart from May 13, 1992, to November 13, 1992, with Stochastics. The %K line is a 20-day and the %D line is a 5-day. The shaded area marked overbought is above 70%, while the shaded oversold area is below 30%. Higher readings show more strength. (*Source:* Bloomberg L.P.)

that were just set up in the previous example could be ranked by momentum of price movement instead of by the more fundamental interest rate analysis. The more momentum a cross rate had, as measured by an indicator such as a stochastic, the higher would be its rank on the list. Figures 6–4 and 6–5 show stochastics and price for the two most widely followed cross rates, mark-yen and sterling-mark. Again, the top few could be bought, while the bottom ones on the list would be sold. The same caveats for diversification expressed in the preceding example also apply here. Another caution is that some of the cross rates generated may be very illiquid, so another more heavily traded one could be used as a surrogate. Overall, this type of analysis provides a cross-rate trader with a systematic approach to trading that is unavailable in traditional futures instruments.

INVESTING IN THE EXOTICS: ANOTHER LOOK

While we warned earlier in the book of the aberrant behavior of currencies classified as exotic, these currencies can play an important role in certain cross-rate trades, namely yield plays. However, remember that high-yield currencies are that way for a reason. By now, you should recognize how inflation in a country can often

greatly diminish the interest income earned from short-term investments in that currency, either through the forward market (receiving forward points) or through that country's money market
(receiving interest from a deposit account). In exotic currencies,
however, inflation is not the only spoiler. There may be not only economic problems but military and political risk as well.

Yield plays here involve much more of a "buy and hold" approach
than a speculative one. Therefore, cross rates incorporating an exotic
currency may involve analysis analogous with modern portfolio theory.
For the patient and cautious trader, they offer a great deal of potential.
Using a method similar to the currency ranking approach described earlier, the exotic currency trader can first start with interest rate analysis
across various currencies. The next step is to incorporate correlative
studies. For example, a trader could buy a portfolio of high-yield exotics,
and sell a portfolio of similarly behaving low-yield currencies, exotic and
otherwise. To achieve an equivalency between the two portfolios, the

	AUD	CAD	CHF	DEM	DKK	ESP	FIM	FRF	GBP	JPY
AUD	1.000									
CAD	0.217	1.000								
CHF	0.008	−0.078	1.000							
DEM	−0.056	−0.109	0.926	1.000						
DKK	−0.053	−0.138	0.906	0.989	1.000					
ESP	−0.101	−0.160	0.796	0.899	0.915	1.000				
FIM	−0.070	0.097	0.642	0.688	0.696	0.635	1.000			
FRF	−0.046	−0.141	0.927	0.993	0.989	0.915	0.697	1.000		
GBP	0.029	−0.020	0.745	0.833	0.839	0.910	0.612	0.837	1.000	
JPY	−0.086	−0.066	0.584	0.599	0.608	0.543	0.432	0.612	0.484	1.000
IEP	−0.013	−0.184	0.803	0.878	0.874	0.783	0.485	0.866	0.786	0.516
ITL	−0.102	−0.075	0.750	0.870	0.884	0.958	0.607	0.872	0.889	0.503
MYR	0.023	−0.118	0.372	0.431	0.443	0.479	0.321	0.448	0.469	0.412
MXP	0.077	0.044	−0.008	−0.053	−0.053	−0.039	−0.037	−0.039	−0.017	−0.126
NLG	−0.049	−0.109	0.920	0.999	0.990	0.896	0.685	0.992	0.835	0.603
NOK	−0.047	−0.117	0.885	0.979	0.989	0.946	0.684	0.978	0.888	0.588
NZD	0.385	0.092	0.194	0.157	0.180	0.115	0.060	0.164	0.205	0.098
PTE	−0.095	−0.138	0.841	0.934	0.938	0.906	0.641	0.937	0.843	0.607
SEK	−0.054	−0.123	0.889	0.974	0.981	0.940	0.695	0.975	0.883	0.584
THB	−0.086	−0.179	0.499	0.562	0.582	0.564	0.383	0.580	0.530	0.656
ZAR	0.020	−0.031	0.715	0.766	0.776	0.748	0.506	0.758	0.740	0.540

Figure 6–6 Correlation Matrix of Percentage Changes in Foreign Exchange
Prices from October 1990 to November 1992. (*Source:* Ezra Zask Associates, Inc.)

trader requires a high correlation between them. There are numerous ways of measuring correlations between currencies. This type of trading must achieve two things. First, it must spread the basket of high yielders across a span of exotics of varying noncorrelation. When trying to reap the risk-laden returns from troubled or developing economies, the investor wants to spread a portfolio out among as many exotics as possible. Second, this type of trading must hedge the basket of currencies with the sale of a basket that correlates against the first one (beta hedging to portfolio theorists). Thus, profits are earned by capturing the net interest income between the two portfolios.

Garnering interest income out of the exchange rate markets, in one sense, is a safe and conservative approach. Losses here, unlike positioning for a price trend, are finite. Only the interest rate differential can be lost. On the other hand, doing anything with exotics can be risky, and caution should be used in studying correlations for this purpose. Figure 6–6 shows the correlation of changes in foreign exchange

IEP	ITL	MYR	MXP	NLG	NOK	NZD	PTE	SEK	THB	ZAR
1.000										
0.753	1.000									
0.404	0.438	1.000								
−0.003	−0.045	−0.030	1.000							
0.883	0.869	0.433	−0.051	1.000						
0.873	0.925	0.456	−0.038	0.980	1.000					
0.182	0.073	0.134	−0.024	0.160	0.164	1.000				
0.860	0.863	0.516	−0.104	0.933	0.940	0.145	1.000			
0.858	0.917	0.454	−0.042	0.975	0.990	0.162	0.930	1.000		
0.562	0.527	0.404	−0.058	0.565	0.579	0.258	0.571	0.571	1.000	
0.739	0.731	0.288	−0.164	0.768	0.789	0.187	0.750	0.763	0.388	1.000

prices, and is provided by Ezra Zask Associates, which uses this type of trading strategy.

TRIANGULAR TRADING

Another strategy that can be very useful, as well as profitable, is trading currencies that act similarly when plotted against each other. A good example of this strategy can be found in the Nordic currencies. Typically, the Swedish krona and Norwegian kroner trade very similarly, particularly relative to the D-mark. This is because their economies and economic policies are fairly similar. The market generally views Sweden as a more stable and desirable currency to hold, so its currency normally trades a bit stronger relative to the D-mark than Norway's does (see Figure 6–7). The cross is usually just under 1.00.

Yet relationships like that between Sweden and Norway are often put to the test. When this occurs, some excellent trading opportunities can arise. In early winter 1992, both currencies were falling against the mark. As this selling began to reach a climax, discrepancies appeared between the D-mark cross rates, mark-Sweden, and mark-Norway. Sweden should have retained its value better than Norway on a relative scale, but in fact, it was falling faster. At that time, there was a perception that interest rate differentials between the two countries were about to begin a period of change. Because traders might have reasoned that the differentials should remain fairly constant for Sweden and Norway, they could have taken advantage of Sweden's relative weakness compared with Norway. Actually, this is exactly what happened when

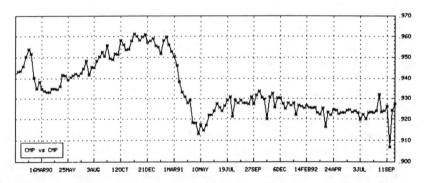

Figure 6–7 Swedish Krona-Norwegian Krone, Weekly Cross-Rate Chart from January 5, 1990, to October 2, 1992. The krona usually trades at a slight premium to the krone. (*Source:* Bloomberg L.P.)

the market quieted down after a couple of days. The mark-Sweden cross rate strengthened against the mark-Norway rate.

Sharp traders could have done two things. They could have bought Sweden against Norway directly or, if they had some opinion on the mark, they might have traded against it. For example, a trader already short the Nordic currencies against the D-mark could have shifted between the crosses as the disparity occurred, that is, decreasing mark-Sweden and increasing mark-Norway. This type of trading is not considered arbitrage, but it is a very profitable way for many cross-rate traders to play the relationships between similar currencies.

ADDING CROSS RATES TO A SYSTEM

Finally, another application for cross-rate trading, and one that is probably the most relevant, is adding crosses to an existing system. The obvious benefits are diversification and sophistication. One of the best things about trading cross rates as part of a trading system is that they trade like currencies or, put differently, trend like currencies. If you are a systems trader or developer, this is an important attribute, because the portfolio enhancement potential for cross rates is very large. In addition to being fairly easy to monitor and trade in a systematic way, the cross rate, if chosen correctly, will also add diversification by having a lower correlation with the rest of a portfolio than would a dollar-based currency.

In addition to diversification benefits, cross-rate trading can add another interesting twist: It may actually tell the trader which markets to trade. For instance, a trader who decides to add cross rates to her existing system may begin trading mark-yen, sterling-mark, and Aussie-yen. Any signals that she gets from her system, she will trade in these markets. However, an interesting twist can be added by following a greater number of cross rates, and only trading those on which a very strong signal is generated. For example, if the system has different strengths for its entry signals, she would only trade those where the strength is very high. So, in effect, the market is determining not only the signals, but also the instrument that is traded.

The next issue is how to actually put on the trade. We can assume that most traders adding cross rates to a system will want to trade them as an independent unit. In other words, if a trader wanted to add sterling-yen to his system, he would trade it as a totally separate position, always entering and exiting the trade as sterling-yen. He would convert his yen profits to dollars either on exiting the position or on a systematic basis, such as once a month. This may seem perfectly obvious, but it is also possible to trade a variation of cross rates that allow "legging" in and out. For example, a trader may put on the sterling-yen cross rate, but get an exit signal on the sterling side only, and maintain his yen position against the dollar. This tactic has several applications, but the most widely used is when the underlying currencies are both in sideways type markets. The trader then puts on a cross rate, and waits for the underlying currencies to break out and establish a trend. Once this happens, one side of the cross is lifted, or legged out of, and the other side is left on as a dollar-based trade. Although this trade is initiated as a cross rate, it is not really considered a pure cross-rate trade within a system.

Another important issue for system traders is historical testing of cross rates. As we discussed in an earlier chapter, data can be hard to find. If the trader is making the switch into the cash markets and is staying with dollar-based trading, he can use the futures market as a surrogate for the cash market. Although this is not the perfect solution, it has advantages in that it is workable and that historical futures price data are easy to obtain. The system trader or developer who realizes the limitations of futures data can still have a reasonable confidence level in the trading results. However, trading cross rates is a different matter. Cash cross rate data in a form suitable for system testing and development is hard to find for the major cross rates, let alone the exotics. One solution is to make a hypothetical cross using ratios in the futures markets. This is a reasonable solution, but it has the same inherent problems that were just discussed. However, it is a good starting place for systems developers. The best solution is to find a data source for cash cross rates or to develop a database yourself. Doing your own development is good because you can track any cross rate and have control over the form of the data. However, the big drawback is that there is no initial historical data to test. On the bright side, more and more data vendors are starting to carry historical data on cash cross rates.

One last point on adding cross-rate trading to systems involves the use of options. Although this text intentionally did not cover strategies for trading options—this is a topic for a complete book—they are well suited for many traders. If an existing trading system utilizes options, cross-rate options should be considered. The OTC variety is very liquid and flexible.

7

WHAT TO EXPECT
IN THE FUTURE

This is a book about cross-currency rates, not U.S. dollar-based exchange rates. Our goal has been to emphasize that for every two currencies in the world there exists, at least in theory, a potential currency market. Although the currency value in U.S. dollars is still very important, and many cross rates are legged into and out of using dollars, the price in dollars is not the sole focus of the world's currency traders.

The general trend of the world's economies, however, appears to point in a direction that may one day make this entire discussion irrelevant. Were all the policymakers and economists to be believed, 30 years from now all the modern industrialized countries of the world will be represented by one of three currencies. Some claim it is not entirely unrealistic to expect one unified currency. In the wake of the Cold War, the industrialized countries now must decide not between two military superpowers but between three large trading blocs. These countries have recognized an intuitive need for exchange rate stability, at least with trading partners. This stability can be obtained either through subtle means, such as a general policy toward maintaining desired levels of exchange, or explicitly, through fixed exchange mechanisms. Today, these countries are divided into three trading blocs: the European bloc, the dollar bloc, and the yen bloc. The European bloc presently consists of the member states of not only the Exchange Rate Mechanism (ERM) but the European Community (EC) overall, and one could even toss in so-called "independents" such as the Scandinavian currencies and the Swiss franc, as well as any emerging eastern European currencies. As of this writing, complete monetary union in Europe is scheduled to be achieved by 1999. This union can be accomplished in either of two ways: (1) by having the European Currency Unit (ECU) achieve the same role as the dollar in the United States, or (2) by keeping the individual units fully intact and interchangeable at some fixed rate. Either way, each state must surrender individual control of its monetary and exchange rate policy. This is a political decision as much as it is an economic one. With turmoil greeting attempts to unify currencies, there is uncertainty about the viability of pan-European currency unit—and of unified currencies in general. Economists have argued for years the merits of the unified ECU and critics have dissented that it will never exist. Although 1999 is the target date for monetary union, it seems that this event will be extended well into the twenty-first century. It must be remembered that this union is highly politicized and that a giant bureaucracy is trying to orchestrate the process. In addition, it can be called into question whether the general populace in Europe is really supportive of union, as evidenced by the furor surrounding vote on the Maastricht Treaty. The Maastricht Treaty outlines the proposed economic and currency union of the European Community. While each Community state has signed the Treaty, it still remains to be ratified by each state. Many individuals do not want their government to give up control of economic policies to some centralized power and may well vote against ratification and economic union of the European states.

It appears that at some future date the critics may be proven wrong, but not due to any success by the ECU. In Europe, the D-mark has asserted itself in this role. Defenders of the ECU, however, may point out one area in which the transnational currency has made some headway—the ECU bond market. The volume of new ECU-denominated issues went from roughly $7 billion in 1986 to nearly $27 billion in 1991, although it has fallen off slightly since. The ECU market's leading bond, a 30-year instrument, is an 8.5% coupon bond issued by France several years ago. Soon afterward, France also issued an 8.5%

10-year note. Both became very popular. Overall, the offerings have largely come from higher-interest rate countries such as France, Italy, Spain, and Britain. Issuing debt denominated in ECUs rather than home currency offers these countries the opportunity to finance at lower interest rates. Even so, many analysts are now predicting some rocky times ahead for the ECU bond market, especially as yields on issues from countries such as Switzerland, Germany, and Holland become more attractive.

The second trading bloc is North America and the Caribbean. Much to the dismay of stalwart and separatist Quebecois, the U.S. dollar may one day unite the financial markets of Canada, Mexico, the United States, and certain other countries. The third bloc is the Pacific Rim, including Japan, the Koreas, and China. Despite express policies in Taiwan and Korea to peg their currencies to the dollar, this trading zone in the future may one day find the yen—the unit most equipped for the job—circulating through the financial straits.

All of this may be decades—and perhaps a century—away. Greek merchants are not going to be funding their purchases in D-marks (nor ECUs) tomorrow. Yet this trend is an important one to keep in mind. Along the path to such a consolidation of world currencies, cross-rate traders should expect many profitable trading opportunities as well as many structural changes.

For example, there should be several new exotic currencies available for trading in the relatively near future as eastern Europe and the former Soviet Union move to market-based economies and join the world economic structure. These countries would benefit immensely from being tied to a currency such as the D-mark, but they must meet strict and specific economic criteria to do so. The bottom line for the European currencies as they move falteringly toward monetary union is that there will still be opportunities for profitable trading for many years to come.

Another trend in the markets has been a movement, especially among money managers, away from the futures market and into the cash market. This is due to several factors, among which are the liquidity in the cash market, the larger number of trading instruments, and the relatively low cost. The futures exchanges are not sitting still. They are constantly looking to attract new business, launch new products, and provide better liquidity. Maybe Globex, or something like it, will be an answer. Many traders love to trade in the cash market but still like the confidentiality of the futures market. An electronic exchange that could provide enough liquidity might be an answer for many traders. One could even argue that the currencies—and cross rates in particular—will be where the futures guys beat the equity guys to the punch. As equity fund managers get more serious about investing in non-U.S. stocks and bonds, they begin trading more currency. Some are now trading currencies outright: billion-dollar fund manager George Soros captured a nice $1 billion or so in late 1992— betting on mark-sterling and other cross rates.

The currency markets, both dollar based and cross based, are one of the most exciting and profitable markets in the world to trade. In recent times, many skeptics have questioned whether or not they will continue to provide profitable trading opportunities. As with all markets, the currencies will have periods of trendless times that are extremely difficult to trade. There will be government intervention to maintain levels or orderly markets, which may also make trading difficult. However, the basic forces that drive economies, and consequently currency prices, will always be with us. If a structural or economic change occurs that will cause the mark-yen to go from 90 to 50, there is no government or other program that will stop it. Because there is no intrinsic value for currencies, as there is in equities or traditional commodity futures such as soybeans or crude oil, they will be able to move into previously uncharted waters with a greater degree of frequency than many other trading instruments. This is especially true as more currencies become available to trade and exchange.

History has shown that the economic powers that survive rely on trade of goods and services. One criterion for the continuance of economic growth on a global basis is the free exchange of currency for the purpose of free trade. As long as this goes on, there should be profitable trading opportunities in cross rates on foreign exchange. We hope that this text has provided the reader with some insight into the cash currency markets in general, and cross rates in particular; and that as opportunities for profitable trading present themselves, it can provide a framework to capitalize on them.

APPENDIX A

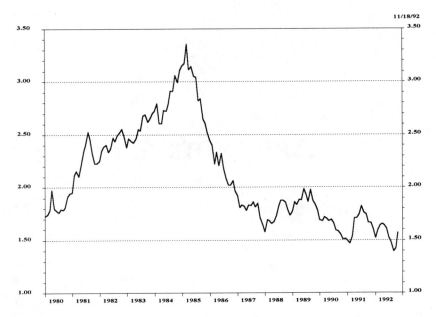

Figure A–1   German Marks per One U.S. Dollar. (*Source:* Datastream International)

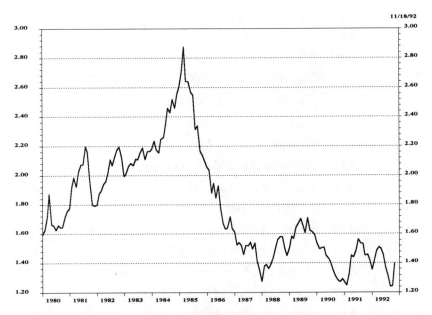

Figure A–2   Swiss Francs per One U.S. Dollar. (*Source:* Datastream International)

Figure A-3   U.S. Dollars per One British Pound. (*Source:* Datastream International)

Figure A-4   Japanese Yen per One U.S. Dollar. (*Source:* Datastream International)

Figure A–5 Canadian Dollars per One U.S. Dollar. (*Source:* Datastream International)

Figure A–6 U.S. Dollars per One Australian Dollar. (*Source:* Datastream International)

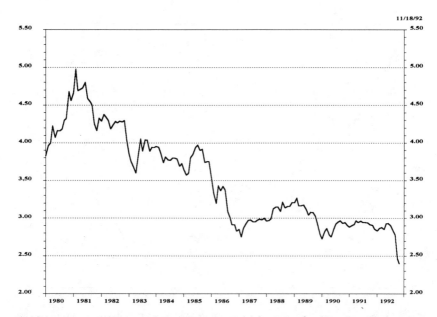

Figure A–7 German Marks per One British Pound. (*Source:* Datastream International)

Figure A–8 Japanese Yen per One German Mark. (*Source:* Datastream International)

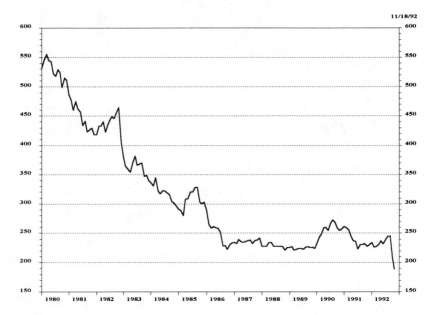

Figure A-9 Japanese Yen per One British Pound. (*Source:* Datastream International)

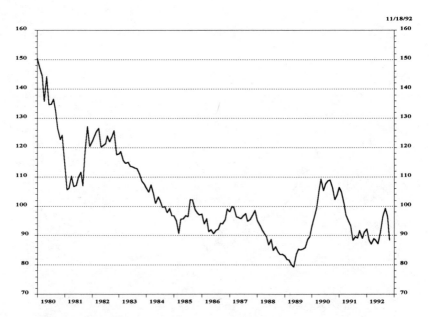

Figure A-10 Japanese Yen per One Swiss Franc. (*Source:* Datastream International)

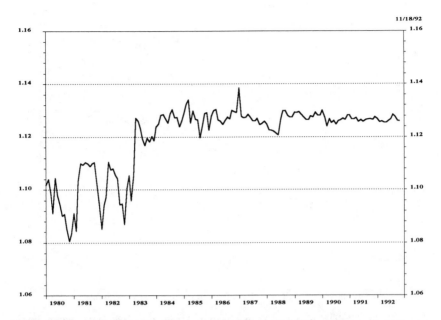

Figure A–11 Netherland Guilders per One German Mark. (*Source:* Datastream International)

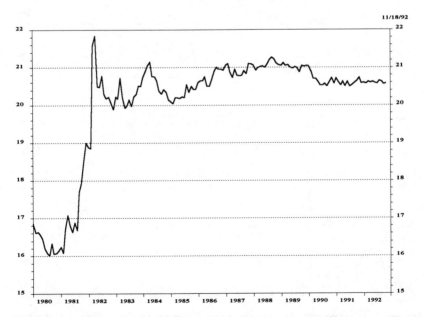

Figure A–12 Belgian Financial Francs per One German Mark. (*Source:* Datastream International)

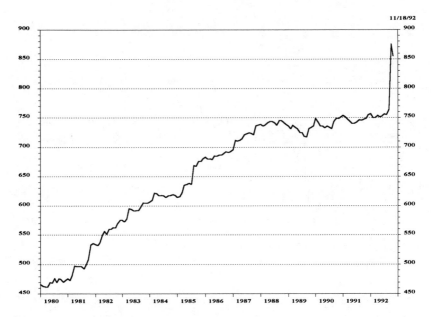

Figure A–13 Italian Lire per One German Mark. (*Source:* Datastream International)

Figure A–14 Spanish Peseta per One German Mark. (*Source:* Datastream International)

Figure A–15 **Swedish Krona per One German Mark.** (*Source:* Datastream International)

Figure A–16 **Norwegian Krone per One German Mark.** (*Source:* Datastream International)

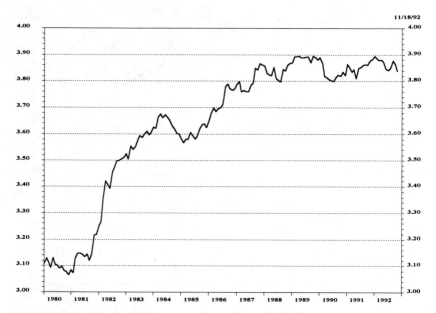

Figure A–17 Danish Krone per One German Mark. (*Source:* Datastream International)

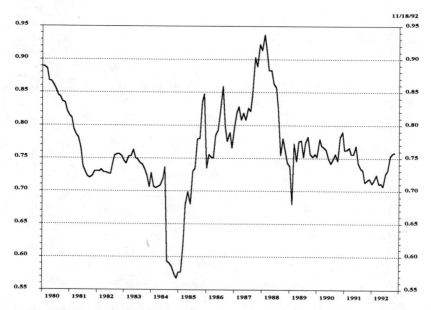

Figure A–18 Australian Dollars per One New Zealand Dollar. (*Source:* Datastream International)

Figure A–19   Japanese Yen per One Australian Dollar. (*Source:* Datastream International)

APPENDIX B

DISTRIBUTIONS OF INTERBANK TRADING

Percentage Distribution of Turnover by Major Currency Pairs (monthly gross, US trading only)

Dollar-mark	34.26%
Dollar-yen	23.44%
Dollar-sterling	9.19%
Dollar-Swiss	7.84%
Mark-yen	2.91%
Dollar-French	2.71%
Sterling-mark	2.23%
Mark-Swiss	2.09%
Dollar-Aussie	1.93%
Dollar-ECU	.83%
Mark-French	.58%
Sterling-yen	.12%
Other	11.87%

Percentage Distribution of Turnover by Type of Transaction (monthly gross, US trading only)

Financial Institutions
Spot	49.25%
Forwards	7.09%

Swaps	30.48%
Options(OTC)	7.60%
Derivatives	5.58%

Brokers

Spot	49.20%
Forwards	.08%
Swaps	37.68%
Options(OTC)	12.31%
Other	.73%

Average Deal Size (1992)

As Reported By:

Financial Institutions	$ 6 million
Brokers	$ 7 million

By Transaction Type

Spot

Financial Institutions	$ 4 million
Brokers	$ 4 million

Forward

Financial Institutions	$ 4 million
Brokers	$23 million

Swaps

Financial Institutions	$16 million
Brokers	$32 million

Options

Financial Institutions	$14 million
Brokers	$40 million

This information is excerpted from "Summary of Results of the U.S. Foreign Exchange Market Turnover Survey Conducted in April 1992 By the Federal Reserve Bank of New York."

GLOSSARY

AMERICAN STYLE OPTION   A contract that gives the holder the right to purchase from, or sell to, the writer of the option a specified amount of a currency, at a stated price. The contact is good for a specified period of time and may be exercised at *any time* up to its expiration (compare European Style option).

APPRECIATION   An increase in the market value of a currency compared with a second currency or asset.

ARBITRAGE   The simultaneous purchase and sale or lending and borrowing of two equivalent assets in order to profit from a temporary price disparity.

ASSIGNMENT   The transfer of the right to receive loan principal and interest or other kinds of payment from a debtor.

AT THE MONEY   A term describing an option whose strike price is equal (or almost equal) to the current market price of the asset on which the option is written.

BACKWARDATION   A relationship in which spot or cash prices are higher than futures (or forward) prices.

BANK FOR INTERNATIONAL SETTLEMENTS (BIS)   Founded during the German monetary crises of the late 1920s, this bank, located in Basel, Switzerland, serves as a forum for monetary cooperation among the major central banks of the industrialized world. It monitors and collects data on international banking activity and serves as a clearing agent for the European Monetary System.

BASIS   The cash or spot price minus the futures price.

BASIS POINT   One-hundredth of a percentage point (.0001).

BID   The price at which a marketmaker in an asset will buy the asset.

BROKER   An individual who matches buy and sell orders in return for a commission. A broker, in contrast to a marketmaker, does not buy or sell for his or her own account and hence does not ordinarily risk the firm's capital in order to stand behind a price quotation.

CALL OPTION   A contract giving the holder the right, but not the obligation, to buy an asset at a stated strike price on or before a stated date.

CAPITAL ACCOUNT   Those items in the balance of payments showing net changes in the domestic private sector's holdings of foreign financial assets or in foreign holdings of domestic financial assets.

CARRY MARKET   A currency market where there is a differential between the interest rates of the currency that is owned and the one that is borrowed.

CARRYING COST   In the currency market, the cost of holding a currency. This cost is a function of the interest rate differential between the currency that is owned and the currency that is borrowed.

CHICAGO BOARD OPTIONS EXCHANGE (CBOE)   An options exchange sponsored by the Chicago Board of Trade (CBOT) and registered with appropriate regulators to trade standardized options contracts through the Options Clearing Corporation.

COLLATERAL   An obligation, security, cash, or asset provided in conjunction with another obligation to secure its performance.

COMMODITIES FUTURES TRADING COMMISSION (CFTC)   A U.S. regulatory body that regulates all exchange-based futures trading in the United States. Established by the Commodities Futures Trading Commission Act of 1974.

CONTANGO   A relationship in which spot or cash prices are lower than futures (or forward) prices (see backwardation).

CONVERTIBILITY   The ability to exchange a currency free of government controls or restrictions. Convertibility in capital accounts means freedom to exchange currency for direct investment for trade in financial assets.

COUNTERPARTY   The entity that takes the liability of the other side of a currency trade.

COUNTERPARTY RISK   The risk associated with a counterparty defaulting on its obligations.

COUPON   The periodic interest payment on a bond. Many bond certificates come with literally detachable coupons that must be removed and presented for payment, usually annually or semiannually.

CREDIT LINE   The maximum amount of foreign exchange exposure a financial institution will allow a client to take.

CREDIT RISK   A risk existing in financial transactions where there is an exposure to receiving cash flows from another party.

CROSS-HEDGING   The hedging of an asset with a futures contract of a different asset.

CROSS RATE   An exchange rate between two currencies.

CURRENT ACCOUNT   Those items in the balance of payments involving imports and exports of goods and services as well as unilateral transfers (gifts).

EUROPEAN STYLE OPTION   A contract that gives the holder the right to purchase from, or sell to, the writer of the option a specified amount of a currency, at a stated price. The contract is good for a specified period of time and may be exercised *only* on its maturity date (compare American Style option).

EX ANTE REAL INTEREST RATE   See Real Interest Rate.

EXPECTATIONS THEORY   The concept that the market moves in accordance to what participants are *expecting,* rather than what is actually happening.

EXOTIC CURRENCY   Any currency that is not a major currency, minor currency, or member of the European Community.

DEPRECIATION   A decrease in the market value of a currency with respect to a second currency or a real asset. The term is used in reference to a market price as opposed to an official price or par value.

DELTA   The ratio of a change in the option price to a small change in the price of the asset on which the option is written; the partial derivative of the option price with respect to the price of the underlying asset. Futures Delta is the ratio of a change in the futures price to a small change in the spot price.

DEVALUATION   A decrease in the official value of a currency with respect to a second currency or a real asset. The term is used in reference to an official price, such as a fixed exchange rate or a declared par value, as opposed to a market price (compare Depreciation).

EXERCISE (STRIKE) PRICE   As related to options, the price at which the option is exercisable.

FEDERAL FUNDS   Deposits held by commercial banks at the Federal Reserve System. The federal funds market is the interbank market for borrowing and lending these deposits. Since reserve requirements of commercial banks with deposits in excess of required reserves will lend the excess deposits to banks with a reserve shortage, at a market-determined interest rate, it is called the federal funds rate.

FLOATING RATE   An exchange rate whose value is not constrained by central bank intervention to remain within a fixed range.

FORWARD   Foreign currency traded for settlement beyond two working or business days from the current date.

FORWARD DISCOUNT   Phrase used to describe a currency whose forward price is cheaper than its spot price.

FORWARD RATE AGREEMENT (FRA)   A forward contract for borrowing or lending at a stated interest rate over a stated time interval that begins at sometime in the future.

FUTURES COMMISSION MERCHANT (FCM)   A firm that is registered with the CFTC and legally authorized to solicit or accept orders from the public for the purchase or sale of futures contracts. It acts as an intermediary between a public customer and a floor broker.

FUTURES CONTRACT   An obligation incurred pursuant to the rules of the futures exchange resulting in daily cash flows that occur with changes in the futures price. If held until expiration, the futures contract may involve accepting (if long) or delivering (if short) the asset on which the futures price is based.

HEDGING   The process of reducing the variation in the value (from price fluctuations) of a total portfolio. Hedging is accomplished by adding to an original portfolio items such as spot assets or liabilities, forward contracts, futures contracts, or options contracts in such a way that the total variation of the new portfolio is smaller than that of the original portfolio.

INTERNATIONAL MONETARY FUND (IMF)   Organization founded at Bretton Woods in July 1944, and located in Washington, D.C., with the goal of overseeing exchange arrangements and lending foreign currency reserves to members. Members were pledged to eliminate exchange controls; they agreed not to alter the exchange values of their currencies without IMF approval, except once by an amount not greater than 10%; members could borrow reserves from the IMF, subject to conditions imposed by the IMF. The IMF obtains funds to lend through member subscriptions. These are usually paid 25% in gold and U.S. dollars and 75% in the members' own currency.

INTERNATIONAL MONEY MARKET OF THE CHICAGO MERCANTILE EXCHANGE (IMM)   The world's largest market for foreign currency and Eurodollar futures trading.

IMPLIED CEILING   The price that a currency cannot trade above relative to another currency, because of an existing fixed exchange agreement that both currencies participate in with a third currency.

IMPLIED FLOOR   The price that a currency cannot trade below relative to another currency, because of an existing fixed exchange agreement that both currencies participate in with a third currency.

IMPLIED FORWARD RATE   The rate of interest at which a borrowing or a lending transaction of a shorter maturity may be rolled over to yield to equivalent interest rate with a borrowing or a lending transaction of longer maturity.

INTEREST RATE PARITY   An equilibrium condition under which a borrower (lender) is indifferent between borrowing (lending) in the domestic currency or in the foreign currency, taking into account the need to convert currency now through the spot market, with exchange risk covered by a reverse transaction through the forward market. A restatement of the interest parity condition yields the forward exchange rate as a function of the spot rate and the interest rates on the two currencies.

IN THE MONEY   A term used to refer to a call option whose strike price is below, or to a put option whose strike price is above, the current price of the asset on which the option is written.

INITIAL MARGIN   The minimum deposit of futures exchange from customers for each futures contract in which a customer has a net long or short position.

INTERVENTION   The process by which Central Banks participate in the foreign exchange markets to control prices.

LETTER OF CREDIT (LC)   A credit facility by which a bank extends credit in the name of a customer, to another bank.

LINE OF CREDIT   See Credit Line.

MAASTRICHT TREATY   A treaty developed in Maastricht, Holland, that deals with the proposed economic and monetary union of the European Community. Each community state has signed the treaty, but ratification—the next step—is not complete.

MAJOR CURRENCY   The D-mark, Swiss franc, British Pound, and Japanese yen.

MARGIN   The equity required to collateralize a position.

MINOR CURRENCY   The Canadian dollar and Australian dollar.

NEGATIVE CARRY   The situation that exists when the currency that is owned has a lower interest rate than the one that is being borrowed.

NOVATION   When more than one currency payment is due on the same day, a provision for the cancellation of those trades and the substitution of one net payment.

OUT OF THE MONEY   A term used to describe a call option (put option) whose strike price is above (below) the current market price of the asset on which the option is written.

OVER-THE-COUNTER (OTC)   Not exchange-traded.

PARITY GRID   A system of fixed bilateral par values in the European Monetary System. The central banks of both countries whose currencies are involved in an exchange rate are required to intervene in the foreign exchange market to maintain market rates within a range defined by an upper and a lower band around the par value.

PIP A term used in the cash currency market meaning one point.

POSITIVE CARRY The situation that exists when the currency that is owned has a higher interest rate than the one that is being borrowed.

PREMIUM The price of an option agreed upon between the buyer and writer or their agents in a transaction on the floor of an exchange.

PURCHASING POWER The value of a currency expressed in terms of its exchange value against a basket of goods and services.

PURCHASING POWER PARITY (PPP) The notion that, all other things equal, the exchange rate for any two currencies should reflect exactly the relative purchasing powers of the two currencies.

PUT OPTION A contract giving the purchaser the right, but not the obligation, to sell a particular asset at a stated strike price on or before a stated date.

REALIGNMENT The process by which currency prices are adjusted up or down within a fixed exchange rate system.

REAL INTEREST RATE The market interest rate as commonly quoted (the Nominal Interest Rate) minus the annualized rate of inflation for that country. The Ex Ante Real Rate is calculated by subtracting expected inflation, while the Ex Post Real Rate is calculated by subtracting actual inflation.

SPOT PRICE The price of currency for two-day delivery; also known as cash price.

SWAP In the interbank currency market, a contract entered into by two parties to deliver a sum of money in one currency against a sum of money in another currency at stated intervals or according to otherwise stated conditions.

YIELD CURVE A graphical representation of the relationship between yield and maturity for equivalent instruments.

YIELD SPREAD The difference in yields between instruments that have either a different issuer or a different maturity.

INDEX